It's Not About You

Understanding Adoptee Search, Reunion, and Open Adoption

An Anthology for Birth and Adoptive Parents, and their Therapists

It's Not About You

Understanding Adoptee Search, Reunion, and Open Adoption

An Anthology for Birth and Adoptive Parents, and their Therapists

Edited by Brooke Randolph, LMHC

Entourage Publishing 2016

Entourage Publishing
www.Entourage-Publishing.com
Ann Arbor, MI

It's Not About You
Edited and compiled by Brooke Randolph, LMHC

Entourage Publishing, 2017
E-book eISBN: 978-1-942312-10-9
Paperback ISBN: 978-1-942312-09-3

Entourage CEO: Laura Dennis
www.Laura-Dennis.com

Cover Art by Linda Boulanger (2017)
TellTaleBookCovers.weebly.com

What People are Saying About
It's Not About You ...

Adoption is often a complex journey replete with angst, despair, joy, wonder, and hope. These narratives offer rare and immeasurable insight into the lives of beautiful individuals shaped by resiliency.

~ Kristin Meekhof, LMSW, Adoptee
Author of *A Widow's Guide to Healing*,
kristinmeekhof.com

* * *

The bravery and inspiration found through these stories are invaluable and underscores the truth that the impacts of adoption truly are lifelong. It's a privilege to hear directly from adoptees in such an unfettered, honest and compassionate way.

~ Angela Tucker, Transracial Adoptee
The Adopted Life LLC

* * *

This book contains short personal accounts about searching, reunions and openness in adoption. This compilation conveys the wide range of emotions involved for all of those touched by adoption. Designed to give a voice to the many different perspectives of open adoption, this collection features guest offerings by adoptees, birth parents, adoptive parents and professionals working in the field. Painful, personal, candid and beautiful, these stories will give one a deeper understanding of what searching, reunions and open adoption looks like, allowing one to appreciate the many brushstrokes that comprise a family portrait. Always, the child is placed at the heart of the text. Overall, open adoption can be a wonderful experience for everyone involved in the process.

This is an essential text for experienced adoption workers or those currently in training. Bottom Line: I highly recommend this poignant and sobering book to others and feel that it should be required reading for adoptive parents, prospective adoptive parents or anyone working in the field of adoption or the child welfare system.

~ Wayne D. Duehn, Ph. D.
Professor Emeritus of Social Work
The University of Texas at Arlington

Dedicated to each author who undertook this labor of love with me. You are inspiring and I am thankful to have you in my tribe. Thank you for sharing your story, your heart, and your knowledge. I am proud of what we have created together.

Contents

Introduction

Brooke Randolph, LMHC

Brooke Randolph, LMHC, is a wife, parent, grandparent, therapist, and adoption professional with twenty-five years of experience working with children, families, and individuals. Her private practice, based in Indianapolis, Indiana, focuses on individual and relationship therapy. Brooke was the mental health expert contributor at DietsInReview.com, a national diet and fitness column from 2008-2015, and a founding member of MLJ Adoptions, Inc., where she served as the VP of Social Services for seven years. She is a Young Professionals Advisory Board member for The Villages, which is Indiana's largest not-for-profit child and family services agency, serving over 1,400 children and their families each day. Brooke adopted an older child internationally as a single woman, which she considers one of the most difficult and most rewarding things she has ever done. She is a contributing author to the book, *Adoption Therapy: Perspectives from Clients and Clinicians on Processing and Healing Post-Adoption Issues* (2014), author of *The Bully Book: A Workbook for Kids Coping with Bullies* (2016), and organizing editor for *It's Not About You: Understanding Adoptee Search, Reunion, & Open Adoption.* She has also authored adoption education materials and presented at numerous conferences and workshops throughout North America on a variety of topics. Brooke is primarily motivated to encourage, equip, and empower individuals and couples toward more whole-hearted living and conscious relationships.

* * *

It is a story as old as time; I saw a need, I even suggested others meet that need, but eventually I realized if it was going to come to fruition, I had to make it happen. This book is a labor of love for me, love for my clients and love for all of those in the adoption triad.

It is an honor for me as a therapist to hear people's stories, to witness their pain, to reflect to them the strength they do not see, to highlight the things they cannot hear themselves saying, to celebrate their milestones and victories, and to help them re-write their "SFDs" ("shitty first draft") as Brené Brown would say. My expertise in adoption came from hearing people's stories. Yes, I have read countless books; attended hours' and hours' worth of conferences, webinars, and presentations; and done plenty of research; but I credit the simple act of listening and seeking out stories to move from knowledge to expertise.

Since before I started graduate school, I wanted to work in adoption. I had always been interested in adoption, and walking with a friend through an unplanned pregnancy, adoption plan, and placement really revealed to me the need for counseling on all sides of adoption. There are not classes on adoption in the graduate programs that train counselors, social workers, and psychologists.

> *When asked how much time they spend discussing adoption in doctoral-level clinical programs, professors reported an average of 7.95 minutes per semester on adoption, yet they reported spending 22.17 minutes on the rare dissociative identity disorder, and 76.82 minutes for schizophrenia (Sass, et al., 2000). I have never seen a case of dissociative identity disorder, but foster care and adoption was something I dealt with at least weekly during my Masters-level internship. Would you want your dentist to have spent ten times the amount of time in school on gum grafts as he or she did on cavities? Would you want your primary care physician to know the ins- and-outs of the rare blood disorder polycythemia vera rather than spending time becoming fully versed in blood pressure or diabetes? (Randolph, 2014)*

While I focused as many of my assignments, papers, research, and interviews as I could around adoption while in graduate school, when I was given the opportunity to help found an adoption agency and serve as Vice-President of Social Services, I knew I needed to know more. Every adoption situation is unique, every story is unique, so I set an intention to learn as much as I could from as many sources as I could.

I have often challenged adoptive parents and prospective adoptive parents to embrace something similar to the personal policy I created. I made it my personal responsibility to hear as many individual stories as I could. I believed the best way that I could advocate for the children involved in the adoption process was to understand their experience, and to do that, I needed to hear from adult adoptees who had lived through adoption. I made it known (publicly through social media) that I wanted to buy a cup of coffee (and often breakfast or lunch) for any adoptee willing to share their story with me, as well as those who were from the various countries where my adoption agency was working because I needed a better understanding of the cultural experiences of the children beyond what I could absorb during my travels.

It was not that it was unimportant for me to hear from adoptive parents or birth parents, but I saw the child as the one needing an advocate. Part of my job was to prepare prospective adoptive parents for adoptive parenting. I felt I needed to be able to represent the experience of the adoptee to create empathy and a better family experience for everyone. As I listened to stories, I suppose I became even more of an advocate for the adoptee. I also realized just how many therapists "didn't get it" and I wanted all adoptees to have access to quality, competent therapeutic services (Randolph, 2014). Today I consider myself an adoptee ally and focus on counseling adult adoptees as one of my specialities.

As a therapist, it is an honor to bear witness to someone's story; sometimes I am the only witness they will allow, and I know my role is sacred. It is from this privilege that this book was formed. I have sat with adoptees struggling to explain to others, particularly their parents, the need for information regarding their biological family. I have often wished for a book that they could hand to their parents that would explain how innate this drive really is. The desire for information has nothing to do with parenting or personality. I have explained this to adoptive parents, yet wished they had a resource to help them feel less alone in their emotional journey through their child's search. I have listened to birth parents who do not know how to process a child searching for them, some fearing judgement. It is from these experiences that this book was born.

As an editor, it is my honor to present to you a variety of stories on the topic of search, reunion, and open adoption, calling on all members of the adoption triad and those involved with both domestic and international adoptions. I present these stories to you, birth and adoptive parents, as comfort; I want you to know, understand, and find peace in the fact that **it's not about you**. Those words, "it's not about you" can be read as snotty or comforting. There are times I wanted to take a birth or adoptive parent by the shoulders, look them in the eyes, and make it clear that **it's not about you,** and you need to quit making it about you because it does not help you or your (adult) child. There are just as many times that I wanted to assure some that **it's not about you** and this drive to search does not mean that you made good choices or bad choices, that your (adult) child sees you as a good parent or a bad parent; you are not evaluated at all, rather this drive is inherent, expected, and natural for all human beings whether adopted or not. The title of this book can be both inflammatory and comforting. I believe different people need to read it different ways. I hope you understand it in the way that is most helpful to you.

It is no secret that I am an adoptive mother. I adopted my son as a single woman through an international pilot program just before he turned six-years-old. Many of the adoptees who contributed to this book have been a parenting support to me in one way or another. They are the ones who understand best what my son may be thinking, feeling, and experiencing. Yes, his story is very unique to him, but adoptees are, in my opinion, the ones best able to check me as a parent and help me understand my son. My family and friends do know my son personally, and I also seek their advice (parenting takes a village, and I am blessed to have an amazing mother, a best friend that is a therapist, and several seasoned moms in my circle). But for certain topics, adoptees have been my first resource and at times my main influence. Often they reassure me more than they check me; these relationships are priceless for me and for my son. April Dinwoodie can tell you how my son stared her down, ogling like he was watching a celebrity, after he found out she was adopted like he was. He has not yet asked 'adoptee-only' questions to anyone, but I am so glad he has these role models in his life.

I fiercely guard my son's story—as it is his story, not mine, to tell. When details about my son's story are pertinent to understanding a situation, I would generally rather speak to an adoptee I know and trust than a therapist. I am a therapist so I know our stringent confidentiality standards, but while therapists are typically very empathetic, I believe adoptees can have a level of empathy and understanding for other adoptees that is rare to any other experience. What I will share about my son's story is that we have what could be defined as an open international adoption, but it feels more semi-open with information shared but very little contact. Mary has a much greater experience with open international adoption which she explains in her chapter. We will travel before he begins puberty and make every attempt to visit with relatives. Approximately annually, I search online for the relatives for which I have names. I did locate someone I believe to be an aunt, but she did not respond to my Facebook messages or friend request. Open adoption is a continuum, but we hope to move further down that continuum in the future. Wendy's chapter has challenged me to at least attempt to seek out an address for this aunt and send a written letter. We are also both planning to do genetic testing; his is primarily for medical information, and I will do it partially as an adoptee ally in case there is any way I can be of assistance in anyone's search.

My father has done a massive amount of genealogical research, so it is possible that I could help make connections even if they are several generations back. My father grew up in a farm house built by his great grandfather with his grandmother literally around the corner. It was a small community, and although it has been close to a decade since my grandfather died, I would not be at all surprised if I could identify myself as "Blaine Randolph's granddaughter" and be welcomed in by most people in that community. My grandfather was a practical farmer that came of age serving in the Army during World War II, so it is not surprising that he did not tell tales of ancestors or seek them out. My father knew his biological family for a few generations, but he wanted to know more, including the exact ethnic origins. I do not think it was too surprising that ethnically we are very Scotch-Irish (confirmed via Ancestry) given the names in our family tree. My father was not raised with that culture specifically, but my father still desired to understand his origins on a deeper level. As a result his grandsons know some Gaelic words and "Molly Malone" was one of the first English songs not on the radio that my son learned to sing. For my father it is about "identity, rootedness, and connectivity" and this is a gift he wishes to pass on to his grandchildren regardless of DNA (Randolph, 2012). He has also happily learned as much as he could about my son's culture of origin and knows more about rugby than anyone else in the family.

Genealogical research is never easy; my parents have had to spend time traveling and researching and putting together scraps of information, but he had access to census information, birth certificates, death certificates, and marriage records. Adoptees generally do not have access to their own birth certificate, the very beginning of the genealogical search. I understand logically why the amended birth certificate was created, as a result of societal thought at the time and to simplify bureaucratic paperwork, but it simply does not make sense any longer; I believe we are well past the time to create an adoption certificate to document adoptions. One thing I learned while editing this book is that amended birth certificates cannot be used to apply for a U.S. passport. I cannot imagine what it must have been like for the person who discovered that he or she was adopted because their birth certificate was rejected by the passport office. I have birth certificates from two different countries stating that I gave birth to my son (I also have an original birth certificate, and he has copies of all three). While I have access to my birth certificate, details like the time I was born never seemed all that important, but you will learn reading this book that for those who do not have access to any true information just how important those details can be.

It is also not just about the adoptee either. I have friends who are the children or grandchildren of adoptees. They also do not have information they would like to have, and they feel cut-off in many ways. They also do not have full medical or ethnic information. Often they feel that they cannot find that information, not just because searching is difficult but because they do not feel it is their search to undertake. As much as they would like to connect to that missing branch of their family tree, they will try to 'protect' their adopted relative by not asking questions and not searching while he or she is still living, making the search that more difficult when it is undertaken if it is undertaken. Yet I wonder how often the adoptee is interested in searching but learned not to talk about it, and they could enjoy searching together if they would only discuss their questions, wishes, and hopes.

As I mentioned, this book is a compilation of different voices telling their own unique stories. You may not relate with all of the voices in this book. If you find a chapter or two that does not resonate well with you, consider skipping ahead, but, please do not close the book. I believe very strongly that there is much to be learned from these stories. There is also much to be enjoyed in these stories. You have a story too, and I invite you to share it with us via #INAYstories We want to learn and celebrate with you also. I would love it if you read this with a highlighter or even a pen to annotate your copy. If you want to argue with us in the margins, that is okay. If you enjoy the book, we want to hear about it, and your Amazon reviews are priceless. You can also tweet at us with #INAYbook.

The voices in this book include people I admire, people I have worked with, people I call friends, and some I am just getting to know. As you read the various voices in this book, please do not read anyone as "angry". You may identify some of us as passionate, but that is different than anger. Lucy did not get what she would have liked from her adoptive parents, but her message is about what adoptive parents in the midst of parenting can do, not blaming her parents. Christina does a wonderful job describing her mixed emotions; the depth and reality of her feelings are so important. While I know it was not easy for her to share, I truly value the gift she has for her expressing herself. Her story is another example of the continuum of open adoption; sometimes information is the most important piece. I am starting this book with Gayle's chapter because it reflects on all of the pieces that I want to include. I hope this book opens the door for you to understand the depth of what adoptee search, reunion, and open adoption is about even if **it is not about you**.

REFERENCES

Randolph, B. E. (2014). Red Flags that a Potential Therapist Could Do More Harm Than Good. In Dennis, L. (Ed). *Adoption Therapy: Perspectives from clients and clinicians on processing and healing post-adoption issues*. Entourage Publishing, Los Angeles.

Randolph, G. B. (2014). *Gifts for my Grandchildren.* Retrieved from https://www.mljadoptions.com/blog/gifts-for-my-grandchildren-20120419.

Sass, D. A., & Henderson, D. B. (2000). Adoption Issues: Preparation of Psychologists and an Evaluation of the Need for Continuing Education. *Journal of Social Distress and the Homeless, 9 (4),* 349-359. DOI: 10.1023/A:1009497927928.

Duality in Adoption

Gayle Swift

An adoptive mother of two now-adult children and a former foster parent, Gayle H. Swift is also a certified coach and co-founder of GIFT (Growing Intentional Families Together). A fifty-year survivor of ovarian cancer, she believes in the joy of the present moment and the blessing of family relationships. In her travels with her family, Gayle has zip-lined in Costa Rica, para-glided in Peru, hiked to the Sun Gate above the citadel of Machu Picchu, and trekked the Mendinhall glacier in Alaska, but parenting proved to be the greatest adventure of her life. She writes two blogs: "Growing Intentional Families Together" (for GIFT Family Services) and *"Writing to Connect,"* which she co-writes with her daughter, Casey. It features book reviews written through an adoption-attuned lens. *Adoptive Families Magazine* named their multi-award-winning book, *ABC, Adoption & Me: A Multicultural Picture Book*, a Favorite Read in 2013. Gayle lives in Florida with her husband and a quirky mini-schnauzer named Shadow.

* * *

Adoption blessed me with two wonderful children. For them, however, the blessing was and is mixed. Adoption creates a lifetime of relationships steeped in duality. Because they belong to both biological and adoptive families, they live in a permanent state of both/and, of co-existing positives and negatives, losses and gains, happiness and grief. Typical of that era, our children's adoptions were closed. Since the late 1980s, another ambivalence emerged in adoption practice: open adoptions began to be offered.

After living with two closed adoptions for twenty plus years, in 2006 our family entered a new stage. My son reconnected with his birth mother. Soon after, our daughter connected with her birth mother as well. We have experienced the pluses and minuses of both closed and open adoption. This helped nurture a strong belief that open adoption is the better choice--in most cases-- with the obvious exception of when family contact endangers a child. Our experience as we journeyed from closed to open adoptions can cast a light on the benefits and challenges to the adoptees, adoptive parents and birth parents.

WHY CHOOSE ADOPTION?

Diagnosed at fifteen-years-old, with ovarian cancer, I had a hysterectomy which ended any possibility of becoming pregnant. I could not conceive (no pun intended) of never being a mom; I knew I would adopt. When I married after graduating college, my husband and I looked to adoption to build our family.

During the twelve-month pre-adoption assessment period, our agency prepared us well by the standards of that time. They educated us to see beyond the myth of adoption as a perfect solution for all involved, one from which all walked away without looking back. They removed the blinders from our eyes and opened our hearts to the birth parents' profound losses. Still, adoption was understood more as an event than as a lifetime journey, even by the professionals. Open adoption was a blip on the horizon of adoption practice and was not offered by our agency. We built our family on an impenetrable foundation of closed-ness and an expectation that love would heal all. Until it became obvious that it didn't.

LIVING IN CLOSED ADOPTIONS

Over the years, we consulted many therapists who operated on the prevailing paradigm. It inaccurately and naively viewed adoption as an event, a "perfect" solution from which all moved forward into the land of happily-ever-after; birth mother moves forward and "forgets"; adoptive family neatly and permanently replaces the birth family. Our suggestion that the children's behavioral issues might stem from adoption stress was quickly quashed, dismissed as preposterous. After all, they were placed as weeks-old infants, what could they be suffering? I sensed they were wrong. Something was going on for my children, something deep, palpable even if vague and formless. My intuition told me their blank slates were not really blank at all. In fact a roiling ocean of emotions, unconscious grief, anger, and disembodied rootlessness plagued them.

Nonetheless, I trusted the "experts" and followed their advice. We encouraged the children to talk about their adoptions, had a well-stocked adoption-themed library, and strove to answer their questions with compassion and to reassure them they were loved. We helped start an adoptive family support group to provide the children and ourselves the friendship of parents and children who like us, lived adoption.

And yet...

They clearly experienced a deep-seated ache that haunted them and carved a void that we could not fill. The children's growing comprehension of their losses-through-adoption created anxiety and generated questions to which we did not have answers. Do you think Mrs. B (the gym teacher) might be my birth mom? Why couldn't a grown lady take care of one little baby? This yearning for answers stirred anger, loneliness, and sadness in them and affected their ability to concentrate at school. Feelings of inadequacy and rejection overwhelmed them; they resorted to conceptualizing their birth parents through a lens of extreme negativity. They justified their birth parents' decisions to relinquish them as bad choices made by evil people. The only alternative their child-minds could form was to blame themselves. I believe in their hearts, they did fault themselves and their negative talk was meant to convince themselves as much as anyone else.

Their belief stood in contrast to our consistent attempts to present their first parents with respect, compassion and empathy. We regularly described adoption as a choice made by adults because of adult problems and an adult's inability to cope. We framed their birth parents' choices as decisions made out of love. In hindsight, this explanation created as much pain as comfort because the inference which the children drew equated love with relinquishment and rejection. This fueled a mistrust of relationships and fears of future rejection by loved ones.

Unusual for the time, at our son's placement we received a single photo of him cuddled in his birth mom's arms. Long blonde hair concealed her face. This photo was no small trinket. He treasured it—as did my husband and I— but the photo, did nothing to alleviate his yearning to know what she looked like, if he resembled her, etc.

On the other hand, my daughter had no photo of her birth mother. This omission cut her deeply; she vacillated between envy, anger and sadness. This disparity in the children's circumstances created a parental dilemma. We certainly could not deny my son the reassurance of this picture but we knew that it would impact his sister negatively. The difference in their experiences created pain for my daughter and built a divide between the children. As parents, it pained us to see her suffer this additional hurt.

Although open adoption is no panacea and has complications also, it does reduce the universe of possibilities down to what is actually true in a specific adoption relationship. My children would not have had to scan every face in the crowd searching for similarities, wondering if it might be a birth parent. As adolescents they would not have had to fear accidentally dating a relative.

In the absence of their specific truth they were left to conjure a variety of scenarios, each uglier than the previous. They began to really understand that most children are not placed for adoption, that before we could adopt them, they had to be surrendered first. In their own words, they experienced adoption as being "given away." Rejected. While they took great pride in our family history, they yearned for and mourned the birth parents and ancestral family they had lost.

Fast forward to the teen years which were agonizing for them—and us—as the children struggled through typical teen identity issues compounded by the complexity of adoption's duality. We were drowning as a family. Therapy proved ineffective. Out of desperation, we turned to residential treatment for my son which worsened the situation.

We agonized, watching helplessly as he soothed his wounds with drugs. We felt impotent and helpless. His hurts were no longer ones we could heal with a hug, a kiss, and a Band-Aid. Platitudes rang hollow. (Your birth mom loved you so much that she chose adoption.) The cure he so desperately needed lay behind the closed door of secrecy and sealed records. Only their birth parents could fill that void. There was no substitute. As much as we loved our children, as much as they were attached to us, we were unable to provide what they needed. We feared for his life.

At the worst point of our lives, our son's birth mother reached out to contact us. He was twenty. Her effort succeeded because the children had been adopted in Connecticut which had a dual-consent policy. (The state operated as intermediary which ensured anonymity until both the birthparent and adoptee agreed.) Her gesture meant everything to my son. Finally, instead of feeling rejected, he felt pursued, special, wanted. We felt like we had received the miracle we had been praying for.

"Her voice felt so familiar…" he told me. Butterflies shivered in my stomach at this simple but powerful evidence of his pining for lost intimacy. This reinforced the reality that while I can be many things to my children, some losses I cannot remediate.

For so long he believed the taunts of kids on the playground and felt "thrown away" like trash. Her reaching out to him affirmed in his mind that he was valued and sought. This provided an important counterbalance to the rejection of having been placed for adoption. His birth mother reentered his life when he was at rock bottom. This reconnection truly began the healing of his losses and enriched his life with an essential relationship.

Adoption provided my children a family to raise them with love but did not eradicate their hunger for connection to their birth parents. Their need was primal, natural and reasonable. It was not indicative of lack of attachment or rejection of us. They needed all of their relationships and both their families' stories.

My husband and I understood this. While they were growing up we actively encouraged our children's interest in reconnecting with their birth families after they turned eighteen. We reassured them we would assist them with the process. Even with this commitment of our hearts and minds, the first time my son referred to his birth mother as "Mom" my heart quivered. A momentary wave of jealousy and insecurity swept over me; I recalled his comment that her voice had felt instantly familiar. *Is this when he will choose her over us?*

I acknowledged these imperfect and very human thoughts, caught my breath, and reset myself to the part of me that knew she was providing the relief and sustenance which he had been craving. I truly did want him to have that. I reminded myself that the years we spent loving and living as a family would not be supplanted by any relationship with birthparents or extended family. My brain knew this was true. My heart feared the worst. *Take a deep breath. Stand with and for him. Trust the love. Be the mother he needs you to be.*

Refocused, I anticipated enlarging the family circle, accepting and embracing any relationships that emerged. My husband and I welcomed them not as competition but as the missing pieces that would help fill the voids which plagued our children's spirits.

LIVING OPEN ADOPTION

No surprise, life is not usually the ideal experience which we conjure in our dreams. Reality both confirmed and contradicted long-held fantasies. Relationships are complicated, especially ones that trigger a realignment of current emotional connections. Like a mobile to which new elements have been attached, the dynamics spun wildly in pursuit of a new balance point.

As my daughter observed the joy and healing which my son's reunion brought him, it awakened her interest in search and reunion with her birthmother. Casey lowered her defenses and dared to initiate a mutual-consent contact request to connect with her birth mother. Naively, she anticipated a fairy tale reunion or at least one as positive as her brother's.

DIFFERENCES IN SIBLING EXPERIENCES OF OPEN ADOPTION

By contrast, my daughter's reunion proved less healing. Although clearly relieved to hear from Casey and learn she was safe and well-adjusted, her birth mother imposed tight restrictions. Contact has been limited to Facebook messaging. Her birth mother cancelled an in-person meeting just hours before it was to have occurred. Casey has braved repeated attempts to meet and/or speak with her birth mother and has received additional rebuffs. Her birth mother never told her family about the baby she bore. At twenty-eight, my wonderful daughter remains—in her own, broken-hearted words—her birth mother's "dirty little secret." Casey recognizes that many of the issues and limitations that led her birth mother to choose adoption persist to this day. Still, this ongoing rejection cuts. Deeply. She continues to hang onto the hope that they can meet, just once, without expectation of a "relationship." She asserts that she has moved beyond wishing for the happily-ever-after and can settle for one, face to face encounter. I listen, comfort, and hope.

LIVING OPEN ADOPTION, THE NEXT STAGE

Both children now see their birth mother as a person instead of a demonized caricature. They understand the factors that precipitated their adoptions, both those resolved by time, as well as those factors which continue. Knowing their birth mothers as adults also helped them imagine a more realistic idea of what life might have been like if they had been raised by their birth parents.

After the initial "honeymoon" of reconnection, reality set in. How does one build a relationship that is primal and essential, yet marred by a twenty-year void with no shared experiences? Mother and child feel viscerally connected. Yet at the same time, they do not "know" one another because they have shared no mutual experiences for two decades. During their years living in a closed adoption, they had thought a lot about their losses and believed they understood them. Now they stand face to face with the reality of being intimate strangers. Grief and loss swirl with added dimension, intensity, and emotion. The permanent duality of adoption means they share DNA, patterns, and quirks but not a history. Those are the chapters which they are writing now.

Reunion places demands on their time. They juggle schedules to arrange time to be together, to develop and enjoy these "new" relationships. Like a jigsaw puzzle with an alternate solution, reunion requires them to incorporate new pieces and create a new picture. It takes emotional energy and courage to work out this new arrangement. Reconnection informs and reshapes identity, alters preconceptions, realigns long-held feelings, forges a sense of continuity and spotlights the

gaps in lost moments they can never get back. Heady
stuff. Tough stuff. Their stuff.

COMPARING POST–REUNION EXPERIENCES

My son, now thirty-years old, recently became a father
himself. He enjoys a warm, accepting and nurturing
relationship with his birth mom. Last year he spent
Christmas with her and finally "met" his extended birth
family—grandparents, aunts, uncles, cousins. They all
welcomed him. This year his mom joined us for
Thanksgiving when she enjoyed meeting her first
grandchild. Abundant blessings for all!

Whether they are children or adults, adoptive siblings
will each have a unique relationship with their birth
parents. This creates potential points for frustration and
conflict, as they compare their respective experiences,
notice discrepancies and work to balance any feelings of
envy. Along the thread of duality in adoption, conflicting
feelings can coexist. Happiness for their sibling may
dance with sadness, resentment or relief about their own
birth parent/family relationships.

OPEN ADOPTION AND THE NEXT GENERATION

Open adoption helps the entire adoptive family, beyond
satisfying the primal need for answers, nurturing identity
formation and providing knowledge of ancestry.
Connection, "belonging" and rootedness flow not only to
the adoptee but also to the future generations. We have

experienced this first-hand as we watched our son introduce his birth mom to his four-month-old son.

We all engaged in the proverbial conversations of attributing the baby's characteristics to his beaming parents: Mom's cheeks, Dad's feet, etc. The conversation extended beyond that to identify similarities with maternal and paternal aunts, uncles, cousins, grandparents. In a closed adoption, this conversation would have been far less rich and limited to one half of the baby's family tree. The other half would have been hidden behind the wall of his father's sealed files.

Fortunately, because our son had reconnected with his mother, he too could enjoy hearing how his tiny son embodied the thread of his biological inheritance. What fun it was for all of us! This connection across generations is powerful, stabilizing and reassuring. It also provided a cautionary tale as family patterns revealed potential inclinations and health risks that must be considered. This knowledge surely benefits the generations yet to come.

SETTING BOUNDARIES

Setting boundaries in open adoption becomes pivotally important as families try to parse the separate and unique birth family relationships of each of their children. Many of us adoptive parents understand how conflicting emotions can coexist as we recall how we felt challenged to celebrate the pregnancies of friends and families while we dealt with our own infertility or awaited a long-delayed adoption referral. In families like ours which include more than one adoptee, relationships with their individual birth family will differ in scope or frequency of contact. This will likely produce comparisons and possible conflict between the siblings—even after they become adults. During their childhoods, a photograph embodied the disparity for my children. Now difference shows up in the level of connection. Nonetheless we cannot deny one a robust birth family relationship because we wish to shelter our other child from sadness or pain. What we want to do as parents is help them face the facts of their story, not whitewash or redact it. If one child has less contact or even none at all, work with them to integrate this challenge. Validate their loss and do not minimize it.

Their circumstances are their personal truth and it is incumbent on us to support them through the realities, not to protect them from their truth. Whenever we resort to incomplete truth, white-washing or omission, we set in place a powder keg that will explode in our faces when our child learns the truth. When such a breach in honesty is revealed, it undermines the child's trust in their parents and leaves their entire lives open to scrutiny and mistrust as they attempt to decipher what else parents lied about. Parents must help adoptees learn to cope and understand and accept the reality of their story. Tell their story in age appropriate pieces that lay the groundwork for revealing fuller elements of any difficult or painful information.

Children will always compare and contrast the differences in their open adoption experiences, what is present, absent, what they wish was present or are relieved is absent, and every emotion in between. Families must understand that disparities will continue throughout their children's lives. In fact, it will follow them into adulthood. Open adoption must adapt over time to reflect the evolving realities of the individual participants.

Important relationships take intentionality, commitment and effort to sustain. Open adoption notches up the intensity and complexity. Over time, the challenges resulting from open adoption will vary in complexity, importance and intensity. During their children's childhood, adoptive parents will be the gate keepers who establish, facilitate and adjust the level of contact between child and birth parent/family. Parents are called to the highest level of integrity in maintaining these boundaries and honoring any promises made to a birth parent prior to placement.

Adoptive parents must do a "gut check" whenever they decide to alter contact. It is imperative to be intentional and scrupulous about this. Scrutinize motives to ensure that any change is made in the best interest of the child. Unconscious factors can influence choices and tempt parents to make decisions based on what is easier or more comfortable for them and/or to protect against any personal angst, pain, or emotional fallout resulting from infertility. Parents may fear that birth parent contact will undermine attachment or compete with the child's affections. They may even worry that the child will prefer the birth parent or might want to move back with them. Both parents—birth and adoptive—as well as the children have complex emotions entangled in adoption that arise from the reality that each experiences both loss and gain. Respectful honesty is essential. The challenges remain present throughout the adoptee's entire lifetime.

Set your internal compass to operate as a team not as rivals.

IN SUMMARY

In balance, I think the benefits of open adoption outweigh the very real challenges. Certainly, our children are entitled to know where and who they come from as they walk through life and strive to become their best selves. Now adults, they get to determine how they will participate in relationship with their birth mothers. Our parental role evolves to be more about support than management.

Undeniably, adoptive parents will have attachments to certain fears, worries or concerns. We must strive to always meet the highest standards of what is best for our child. Examine your motives. Before we make decisions we should ask ourselves: *Is this best for my child? Or is it about making the situation easier for us as parents?*

Prior to adoption we had a "pre-existing" family. We knew the dynamics of maintaining relationships as a spouse or significant other can be intensely challenging. Being in relationship with birth parents and birth family is fraught with intense emotions for each person. This makes it exponentially challenging and absolutely worth it for our child. Acknowledge that it is difficult and commit to handling any land mines as they arise. Consider Mother Theresa's words, *"We think sometimes that poverty is only being hungry, naked and homeless. The poverty of being unwanted, unloved and uncared for is the greatest poverty. We must start in our own homes to remedy this kind of poverty."* The sustenance that grows from connection to their birth parents and birth families, nurtures their hearts, minds and spirits. We have the power to choose that.

Many adoptive parents understand how conflicting emotions can coexist because they recall how they felt challenged to celebrate the pregnancies of friends and families while they dealt with their own infertility or awaited an adoption referral.

It would be unfair to deny one child birth family relationships because they are unavailable to their sibling. This would be counterproductive, cruel and deceitful. I can almost guarantee that eventually the truth will emerge. When it does, this breach in integrity will significantly damage the parent/child relationship, undermine the child's trust in their parents, open their entire lives to scrutiny and, leave them to wonder what else their parents lied about. Instead, nurture each child's birth family contact as fully as possible. Help each child learn to cope, understand and accept the reality of their story. When one child has less contact or even none at all, work with them to integrate this challenge. Validate their loss and do not minimize it.

In our family, we continue to support our children as they straddle the disparities in their stories. We talk about the differences and discuss how they feel about them. For our lifetime, we will be their parents. For their lifetime, they will continue to need their families—both of them.

Part I

Search & Reunion

Who's Afraid of the Big Bad Birth Mom?

Deesha Philyaw

Deesha Philyaw is a Pittsburgh-based freelance writer who writes about race, gender, parenting, and pop culture. Along with her ex-husband, she is the co-founder of co-parenting101.org and the co-author of *Co-Parenting 101: Helping Your Children Thrive in Two Households After Divorce.* Her publication credits include *The New York Times, The Washington Post, and The Pittsburgh Post-Gazette; Stepmom, Essence, Brevity,* and *Bitch* magazines; and anthologies such as *When We Were Free to Be: Looking Back at a Children's Classic and the Difference It Made; Motherhood Memoirs: Mothers Creating/Writing Lives; Literary Mama: Reading for the Maternally Inclined*; and *The Cassoulet Saved Our Marriage: True Tales of Food, Family, and How We Learn to Eat.* Deesha is originally from Jacksonville, Florida. She graduated from Yale in 1993 with a BA in Economics, and she also holds an MA in Teaching from Manhattanville College. She is a Fellow at the Kimbilio Center for African American Fiction. Deesha has hit the mama trifecta: She is an adoptive mom, a biological mom, and a stepmom of four daughters.

* * *

My ex-husband and I adopted our youngest daughter Peyton, age twelve, when she was two-weeks-old. Peyton's experience of her adoption is separate from and interwoven with my experience as her adoptive mother. We each have a right to tell our story, but as a writer who writes frequently about parenting, I try to be mindful of where my story ends and Peyton's begins. This kind of "what's hers/what's mine" thinking also helps untangle us so that I can support her desire to meet her birth mother someday.

I am not an adoptee. My mother gave birth to me and raised me. My father was in and out of my life, but I knew who he was. Everything I know about the experience of being adopted, I have learned from Peyton, other adoptees, and others who were not raised by a biological parent. Both my husband and my ex-husband grew up without their biological fathers. Peyton's stepmom is also an adoptee. So I am surrounded by people who have varying degrees of longing and interest in learning more about the parents who did not raise them, including Peyton.

Still I do not know what it is like to have been raised by someone other than the person who gave birth to me. I do not know what it is like to wonder about a father I have never met. Perhaps I have a better idea of this than the average person, but still I don't know. And for this reason, I try to maintain a learning and listening posture when Peyton expresses her desire to learn more about her birth family and to meet her birth mother. I try to use language that reflects the limits of my knowledge. My knee-jerk "I understand that..." becomes "I know it is very important to you that…"

The idea of this book appeals to Peyton. She likes that there will be a guide to help adoptive parents and birth parents see beyond their own feelings in order to better support their children through the search and reunion processes. But my intention here is still to tell my story primarily, to share my feelings about Peyton's desire to meet her birth mother. "Feeling," singular, would be more accurate. Because ever since Peyton first discovered ancestry.com a few years ago, and got the idea to look up her birth family, I have had a single overarching feeling: fear.

I am not afraid of losing Peyton. I do not feel threatened by the idea of her meeting her birth mother. I don't interpret her intention to meet her birth mother as a show of ingratitude. This desire on her part does not make me feel inadequate or unappreciated as a mother. The truth is, I have felt, at times, inadequate and unappreciated long before now, through all the many years that Peyton has been able to express a longing and mourning for her birth mother. Perhaps this is why I was not shocked or hurt when a few years ago, Peyton casually asked me for her birth mother's last name so that she could look up her family on ancestry.com. People who are not familiar with adoption (and even some who are) are baffled that

Peyton, adopted intraracially at such a young age, is interested in her origins, but I have never questioned her interest and feelings about this. I have accepted them, and this was my very first lesson in **"This isn't about me."**

Expecting to be "enough" mother for Peyton is like expecting to quench her thirst with a glass of berries, instead of water when her throat is parched. Sure, berries are refreshing, but she wants water. I have tried over the years to understand her thirst, to see all the ways she loves me very much and has bonded with me, even as she yearns for the mother she has not known. And I want her to be reunited with her birth mother when she is an adult because I know just how long and just how much she has wanted this. I know that this is a question to which she feels she needs an answer in order to have peace. Recognizing that my child has lost something irreplaceable, helps me to understand how important reunion is to her—and that **it's not about me.**

So my fear is not that Peyton will meet her birth mother and reject me. My fear is that the reunion will not give Peyton what she is longing for, that it will not go as she imagines. My fear is that, instead of healing the hurt she has carried for so long, a fresh wound will be opened. But I keep this fear to myself, mostly. I have talked to Peyton about the mixed experiences of adults I know who have searched and been reunited with one or more of their birth parents. I try to sound matter-of-fact about it; I don't use the language of fear because I do not want to discourage or paralyze Peyton. I also do not want her to feel guilty about wanting to search or that she is somehow betraying me by doing so.

Our adoption agreement stipulates that Peyton's birth mother is open to contact once Peyton turns 18. So I have at least a few years to deal with my fear and to figure out how to support Peyton when she begins the search and reunion process. In the meantime, Peyton wants to look up her birth family on ancestry.com, "Just to look," she says, not to contact her birth mother. I have used the following analogy for why I cannot allow her to do it: "Giving you her last name while you are still a kid is like handing you the keys to my car. Sure you might just hold the keys (i.e., just look on ancestry.com). But you could decide to try and drive, and that would be very risky. You might drive just down the street to your dad's house perfectly fine...or you could crash. I love you, I want to protect you, and I cannot take those kinds of chances."

Let's take the driving analogy a step farther. Not wanting Peyton to meet her birth mother at all would be the equivalent of not wanting her to drive even when she is of age because I am afraid she will get into an accident, or that she will drive away from me. This idea, however irrational, has some appeal. It is human. But it is also selfish and offers a false sense of security.

One of the most heartbreaking lessons of parenting is that we cannot protect our children completely. We cannot spare them disappointment or heartache. They will have some wounds that we cannot heal. They will take journeys to places we do not want them to go but that they feel they must go in order to be whole or satisfied. This may leave us as parents with hurt feelings of not being enough for them, but it is not our children's jobs to protect us from the hard truths about who they are and what they need.

As a compromise with Peyton, I have agreed to find out what I can now about her birth family on **ancestry**.com - where they immigrated or migrated from, where they settled, their ethnic mix, and anything else I can share with her. We also plan to send her spit sample away for DNA testing for ancestry.

I am excited to explore my daughter's origins with her. And though my excitement is tempered by fear at the thought of this exploration eventually involving her outreach to her birth mother, I am prepared to be alongside her then too, to whatever degree and in whatever way she needs me to be.

The Journey Before and During the Search

April Dinwoodie & Kimberly Paglino

April Dinwoodie is a nationally recognized thought-leader on adoption and foster care. As Chief Executive of the Donaldson Adoption Institute (DAI), April is committed to improving laws, policies, and practices through sound research, education. and advocacy. She is also a co-founder and Vice President of the Board of Fostering Change for Children, a progressive nonprofit that helps drive innovation in the child welfare system. Before joining DAI, April created a specialized mentoring program called "Adoptment," in which adults who were adopted and/or spent time in foster care serve as mentors to youth in care. As a transracially adopted person, April shares her experiences at workshops and conferences to help potential adoptive parents and professionals understand both the beauty and complexity of adopting children of different race.

Kimberly Paglino is a New Jersey born and raised adopted person. After receiving her Bachelor of Arts degree in Psychology from Loyola University in Baltimore, MD, she went on to earn a Master's degree in

Social Work from Monmouth University in West Long Branch, NJ. Kimberly has past professional experience in the area of child welfare, including as a case worker for the New Jersey Department of Children and Families. She additionally has developed and presented educational seminars for pre- and post-adoptive parents at various adoption agencies and parent groups throughout New Jersey and in New York. She has prior served as an Instructor at Monmouth University, teaching in areas of Social Welfare Policy & Services and Human Rights and Social Justice. Since 2007, Kimberly has been an advocate with the New Jersey Coalition for Adoption Reform and Education (NJ CARE) and has testified for adoptee's rights before the New Jersey State Legislature. She is proud to have been a part of the effort to have enacted the New Jersey Birthright Bill signed into law on May 27, 2014 by Governor Chris Christie, which allows New Jersey adopted persons to access their original birth certificates.

* * *

Reunions between adopted persons and their biological families are popular topics in the news media and on television programming. These sensationalized stories often do not represent the true reality of these complex journeys. It is important that you do not rely on these representations as a template for the search experience; in fact, the real heavy lifting for an adopted person often occurs when they are engaged in the process of deciding whether or not they wish to search.

This part of the journey may not be worthy of a television miniseries, yet it is a critical time when an adopted person needs the support and validation of their loved ones.

An adopted person's decision to search can be just as complex, exhilarating, painful and poignant as the search itself and the possible reunion that may follow. Ultimately, this is a decision that takes a tremendous amount of courage, which is why unconditional support from family and friends is crucial during this time.

THE STATS

One of the first things you can do as an ally for the adopted person in your life is to arm yourself with facts about the experience of search and adoption. This information will not come from the movie of the week or the latest news headline, but reading books and articles about this experience by adopted persons or others who have lived this experience is an important tool for you to be an informed supporter. You should also learn about what the experience of adoption is like today and how it has evolved over time.

When we think about search and reunion today, so much of the activity is surrounding the 'closed' adoption era when very little information was shared between families. Often times adopted people and their adoptive families only received limited information about the adopted person's biological family, as the historical preference was to completely separate the adopted person from their family of origin. Today, we know this is unhealthy for identity development, and current research demonstrates that over 95% of adoptions currently have some form of openness. This often includes members of the biological family and adoptive family developing and maintaining relationships over time. Although this is a process that was recommended for many decades, it was not until the late 1980s and early 1990s, that it started to become more of a commonality.

It is important to remember that while people in open adoption may have access to some more details than those from closed experiences, there are still many who lack basic information about their biological origins for a variety of reasons. Even within the realities of openness in adoption, the majority of states still prevent adopted persons from access to their identifying birth information, including their original birth certificate. For those adopted outside of the U.S., getting information is even more of a challenge. So even though things are shifting, the journey of search is still a common aspect of the adoption experience. Be mindful of these complexities when your loved one is figuring out both the practical and personal aspects of this journey.

THE SPARK

Why does an adopted person decide to search for biological family members? Loved ones often wonder what sparks this need and are frequently left without an answer. The "spark" can happen anywhere and at any time and there is likely a continuum of different factors that play a part. Research and lived experience reveals that everything from significant life events, such as the birth of a first child; major transitions, such as marriage; to simple life moments all influence an adopted person as they think about such an important endeavor. The reality is, the 'spark' that ignites the search has likely burned slowly over time for the adopted person, at times glowing brightly, at other times barely flickering. Most of us typically have a desire to know all parts of what makes us who we are. This is not an adoption need; it is a human need. Considering this journey from a shared human experience will likely enhance your understanding of why this is so important for your loved one.

The experience of being adopted is part of an adopted person's identity. A 2009 Donaldson Adoption Institute report, *Beyond Culture Camp* (McGinnis, Smith, Ryan and Howard), noted that "Adoption is an increasingly significant aspect of identity for adopted people as they age, and remains so even when they are adults." This should come as no surprise to people who are not adopted. Again, in order to love all parts we need to know all parts.

Life events that naturally invite reflection about identity and family, such as weddings and births, may set the stage and open up thoughts about searching for biological family members. At the same time, some adopted people may have very practical reasons that ignite the instinct to search. This may occur in the form of an illness an adopted person experiences personally that creates more questions about one's physical and emotional health and what role genetics may play. Or perhaps a person just becomes tired of never being able to fully complete medical forms at a doctor's office, leaving blank the incessant questions about conditions that run in the family. Hopefully, we have all moved past the debate about whether or not a biological medical history is important. If it was irrelevant, it likely would not comprise the bulk of a 'new patient' packet at every physician's office!

The 'spark' is lit then from a variety of different places. What is important as a friend or ally is that you stay the course, even when it may seem there is very little concrete activity surrounding the actual search. The best place for you in staying the course is side by side with your loved one. You may want to rush them ahead to the finish line, perhaps out of excitement or curiosity yourself. You may also be tempted at times to pull them back, perhaps trying to protect them from disappointment of a negative outcome or because of anxiety surrounding how your relationship may change with your loved one if the search concludes with a reunion. Tempting as it may be to take control, your loved one will appreciate it more in the long run, if you allow him or her to fly the plane. In fact, the most important thing you can do as your loved one contemplates these possibilities is to actively listen without judgment. Sometimes, your loved one will directly communicate with you about their thoughts, worries and needs. Other times, the process may not be so proactively communicated. But if you are truly listening, you can be a significant support throughout the timeline they choose, casting light on their path in small and large ways. Whatever the outcome for the adopted person, one thing that is certain is they will need their existing support system in place, either to add on to or to rely on, as they process this rich journey.

THE STRENGTH

One of the most important things you can remember about the search experience is that it takes guts to consider initiating a search for the family you were born to but not raised with. Strength is a key element of deciding to search and that strength is often about personal power. Frequently, adopted people may feel as though others have dictated their paths without them being able to provide input or direction. While no baby has control of how they come into the world and no one ultimately chooses the family they know, adoption adds layers of complexity, particularly for adopted people that have little to no information about their beginnings. Even as adults, they are confronted with the hard reality that they are regularly denied access to information about themselves and their origins. It is an incredibly disempowering experience when an adopted person requests information from the adoption agency that transacted their adoption and is provided with a packet of information with blacked out or missing names and places. In some states, the actual place an adopted person was born can even be altered! So for many adopted people, even the mere consideration of a search can be extremely empowering and a way to regain control over what can at times feel like a 'limbo' life experience.

What can be difficult for the adopted person is keeping their strength up during this stressful time. For adopted people, it may feel overwhelming to try and regain some control over their life path, yet to know that, like so many other things in our lives, the direction and outcome are ultimately outside our control. The ebb and flow of their interest and motivation to commence a search may feel frustrating for the loved ones that surround the adopted person. It can be worrisome to watch your loved one really struggle with their decision making. It may also feel frustrating for you to observe your loved one as they vacillate in their decision. This is all a normal part of the process and you should not feel pressure to offer answers or guarantee outcomes. The reality is, a search can result in many diverse outcomes. Although your loved one may want to prepare themselves for each and every nuance, they can't. As their support system, all you can do is promise to be there for them regardless of their choice and regardless of the outcome. Be a sounding board for your loved one; do not be afraid to engage in a dialogue about the intricacies of this decision, yet at the same time, make sure you are not offering judgment or taking the reins away.

As a partner in this journey to your loved one that may be considering a search and possible reunion, you will need a reservoir of strength and love to support them. Your loved one will need to be able to rely on what they know as they embark on a voyage to try and resolve the many unknowns about their life. Your consistent and patient presence is the best tool you can provide to help your loved one navigate this path.

THE SCHEDULE

The decision to embark on a search can take a long time, and comes with no set timeline. Some people jump quickly into this process; others may take years to even take a the first step and try to find non identifying background information. If you are not an adopted person, it may be tempting to have a clear cut way of looking at the situation; you may say to yourself 'if it were me, I would just start because times a wastin!'; or perhaps you would say to yourself 'they seem to have it pretty good, why open a can of worms?'. Here though you are offering a perspective on something that is truly difficult to wholly understand unless you have lived the experience yourself. Think about one of the most difficult decisions you have ever had to make, one that not only impacted you in a meaningful and poignant way but also many people you are close to. Think about what informed this important decision. Think about how you ultimately arrived at the decision and who was influential in helping you get there. Think about what action you ultimately took and finally think about the reverberation of your decision on others you love dearly. Think about whether or not there was a set schedule on what you did and when.

Think about whether or not it was ever helpful when someone rushed you, obstructed you, or said something like, "well, if it were me…". The reality is, **this is not about you!** Even if you are an adopted person, and a loved one who is also adopted is deliberating about a search, it is not your story. Although it may feel like similar circumstances, there are many nuances to each individual adoption experience.

Keep in mind also, the amount of support people need for any life altering decision will differ. Each person has a different comfort level surrounding how many people they wish to include. Some people include a large group of people to aid in the process, while others keep things close, only engaging a chosen few. Some do not engage others at all, making the decision completely on their own. Follow the adopted person's lead - if you are asked to aid in their decision to search, the best assistance you can offer is to walk the path with them, not for them. This is an incredibly personal decision, and ultimately one only the individual who is adopted can make.

The process of search and reunion can be very complex and challenging but it can also be a journey filled with positive reflection and necessary healing. Standing with your loved one as he or she moves closer to their decision is a place of privilege. You do not need to have the answers, but ideally you can stand with your loved one as they wrestle with their decision about whether or not to take a very profound journey.

The best advice, for both searcher and supporter, may just be found in the words of Proust, who stated "We don't receive wisdom; we must discover it for ourselves after a journey that no one can take for us or spare us". –Marcel Proust.

IGNITING THE JOURNEY

Just like making the decision to search, the search itself and the many outcomes it holds is a poignant experience for the adopted person and their loved ones. It is vital to remember that just like the pre-search journey, the actual experience of searching is a process. The stories we see about search and reunion show us the end point; rarely do we see what happened leading up to the result. Popular media rarely depicts the many shades of grey that are most likely to constitute a search outcome; rather extreme stories that conclude as a cautionary *or* fairy tale are the frequent headlines seen on this topic. In reality, the more typical search experience dwells somewhere in between these dramatic polarizations.

As you support your loved one in this 'action' period of searching, many of the principles we already discussed in the pre-search stages will apply. What is important to remember in this phase is that there is no specific template or time frame to follow. The road map differs for each person, and within each search, new directions are frequently taken. This is not a linear journey and as more information is revealed, there are many stops and starts. The adopted person may at times feel motivated to take additional steps, and at other times your loved one may pause their efforts. All of this is a normal part of the experience.

Although searching is a distinctive experience, there are some universal themes and guidelines that may help those closest to someone who is searching understand and support the adopted person throughout their unique journey.

THE STATS

There is not an overwhelming amount of research surrounding the issue of search and reunion in adoption, and there is also little empirical knowledge about the process and practicalities of searching. While search has been happening for years and there have been many reunions within the community as a result, much of what we know comes from anecdotal accounts.

What we do know from research is that searching is not uncommon. We also know that healthy identity development for adopted persons includes having access to information about their biological origins; ideally the adopted person will be able to integrate this information with their family of experience in order to have a complete sense of who they are. This is one of the reasons openness in adoption increasingly came to be recommended as best practice. Public opinion today also supports connections between biological and adoptive families. The Donaldson Adoption Institute conducted research that demonstrates more than half of the general public support adoptions where biological and adoptive family members have ongoing relationships with one another.

As we discussed in the previous chapter, adopted people from the closed era of adoption may have more difficulties accessing information about themselves and their biological history. At the same time, we cannot assume that just because an adopted person had an 'open' adoption that they have complete information about their biological family. Search can be a part of this life-long journey no matter when an adoption took place.

As a support person, it is helpful if you continue to arm yourself with facts about the search experience in adoption. Although research is limited, there are ways you can access reliable accounts. What is most important to remember is that search is a normal part of the adoption experience. In fact, it is a normal part of the human experience to need complete information about yourself! This is why websites that explore genealogy or offer DNA testing have become so popular. The adopted person's search journey may be filled with different complexities than the average genealogy buff, but always remember that the need for this information is universal. As a support person, if you can maintain this perspective, it will provide invaluable sustenance to your loved one during this complicated journey.

THE SPARK

Just as there are different motivating factors that first 'spark' interest in searching, there are different motivators that ignite the actual search. These include both emotional and practical starting points that may differ greatly depending on the person and their particular life circumstances.

Keep in mind that what the adopted person feels comfortable articulating about their need to begin a search may only brush the surface of the myriad thoughts and feelings they have as they begin this powerful journey. Your loved one may tell you their search is simply about the practical need for concrete information, such as learning medical background. They may start their search with a carefully typed out sheet of questions to ask about their family health history, similar to a doctor having an initial appointment with a new patient. The difference here is that this is not a professional interaction; rather it is one of the most personal interactions between two people, no matter the practical picture your loved one may be painting. Remember to meet your loved one exactly where they are at in this moment; the adopted person needs to set their own pace with both the practical and emotional steps of their search journey. At the same time, it is important for the adopted person to have a sense of the range of emotions they may experience. When your loved one was deciding whether or not to search, you may have suggested additional supports, such as mutual aid groups that are often led by those connected to adoption. It may be useful for the adopted person to continue to utilize these resources; there is no such thing as too much support during the search process! It is important that your loved one creates spaces where they can prepare themselves and release the different emotions that naturally come up throughout the search experience. As a support person, normalizing this outreach can help increase your loved ones comfort level with creating a network of support to lean on during their journey.

There is also the practical reality of starting a search, which ideally begins with as much information and knowledge as possible. Organizing as many facts as possible at the start of the journey does not guarantee the outcome, but it can set a person up for greater success. A big binder with lots of pockets and sleeves also makes a great gift to someone who is just beginning his or her search. Keep in mind that every state differs in their laws surrounding what information an adopted person is legally allowed. Helping your loved one understand what they are entitled to is a key first step. At the same time, there are more options available to adopted people today than in the past. Advances in DNA testing, for example, have provided more answers than ever before for adopted persons. This has been particularly useful for persons who were adopted from different countries. Remember, there are added layers of complexity in the search for this group of adopted persons, and they often have the greatest difficulty accessing even basic background information. Understanding these nuances and helping your loved one research all of these possibilities based on their unique situation, may be a useful way to provide some practical help at the outset. Remember though to respect your loved one's decisions about what tools they are and are not comfortable using as they learn more about themselves.

There are many questions at the start of the search; some will be questions that have answers and others simply will not. The adopted person's search for their family of origin is often like a puzzle that is built piece by piece over time. As a support person, you can offer to help with these practical elements of information seeking while also providing a listening ear; there will be frustrations throughout, particularly when more questions arise without available answers.

Remember, adopted people are entitled to their truth. There will be many ups and downs along the way, both practical and personal. As a support person, validating your loved ones right to engage in a search in a way that feels comfortable for them, normalizing their desire to search, and offering practical help when needed are all essential elements of starting a search off on the right foot.

THE SCHEDULE

The best way to describe a search schedule is that you may feel at times your loved one is spending more time *not* searching then actively engaged in the process. You may also observe that they spend a lot of time talking about what needs to be done but little time acting on this. Exercising patience and accepting the adopted person's pace will help your loved one feel safe inviting you into this private and personal journey.

The schedule of searching is not linear. With each practical task that is accomplished, the adopted person will experience a range of emotions and their motivation to take additional search steps may fluctuate. During the initial search steps, many adopted people may reach out to the agency or professional that was involved in their adoption. Typically, state laws do allow adopted people to at least be provided with their non-identifying information by the agency that facilitated their adoption (for certain types of private placements this may not be possible). If this information is available, it typically provides very limited details and items such as last names or other identifying facts are not included. However, some adopted people receive this basic background information and then take a long pause from searching further. There are a variety of reasons for this possible break. Your loved one may need to take time to process even what seems to be basic information. This may be the first time in their life they learned simple facts others take for granted, such as the time they were born or what their biological mother's first name was. Your loved one may also have learned difficult details surrounding the circumstances of their birth and placement for adoption.

No matter what they learned, big or small, it is a very significant moment for your loved one. As a support person, your role is to validate the different emotions, welcome dialogue when the adopted person is ready to have it, and normalize reaching out for additional supports as needed.

You can also help your loved one create some organization around this process by encouraging them to take things one step at a time and helping them feel proud of any step they take, however small it may seem. Spending an hour researching the law on what they are entitled to in the state they were born and/or adopted in is a critical initial step. It is okay if weeks or even months go by before your loved one follows this task by sending a letter to request the information they can access. All of these activities should be documented in order to keep track of what has been done and also as a way to journal and process this experience. There is value in your loved one taking time to allow information to settle in, and then move forward with next steps. While it may be tempting and exciting to see things unfold and frustrating when things may stall, it is vital that you allow the person who is searching to be in control of the pace.

At other points, things can move very swiftly. Again, each adopted person is different and so each will handle their search distinctly. As a support person, you still want to continue to validate this pace but it may be a good idea to gently suggest that a pause in the action may be healthy at times, even if it seems like momentum will be lost. Ultimately, these decisions are up to the adopted person alone. As a support person, you may want to think about attending an adoption support group yourself.

Many groups will allow allies and loved ones of adopted people to attend as members of our extended community. You will be surprised at how much wisdom you will gain from doing so.

The schedule of searching is unique to each individual searcher; the pace will ebb and flow, and breaks are a normal and healthy part of the process. Continue to offer both practical and emotional support and always respect the control the adopted person needs to have over this journey. This will help create a valuable partnership between you and your loved one as they navigate this path.

THE STRENGTH

Kicking off a search takes a ton of courage for the adopted person which is why the process can be a long one. The secrecy, stigma and shame that have shadowed the history of adoption create practical challenges in accessing information. Perhaps the greater damage of a closed adoption system is that many adopted people do not feel entitled to ask for even basic details about their original history. At the same time, adopted people have been exposed to a variety of societal perceptions that may suppress your loved one's need to gain information about their biological origins. These include being made to feel 'lucky' for having been adopted, negative presumptions about biological family as incapable or unwilling to parent, and the common misperception that most biological families would not wish to be located by the adopted person.

As a support person, it is important you take careful stock of any existing stigmas or stereotypes you may hold about adoption to make sure you do not intentionally or unintentionally communicate them to your loved one. Listening without judgment and ensuring the adopted person has supports in place no matter the outcome of their search are key elements of being a solid foundation for your loved one during this process. The reality is there is no single outcome in searching. The experience and the results vary widely. Have empathy for the fact that whatever you may be worried about for your loved one, they are even more afraid of the many unknowns that may occur at the end of their quest.

It is important to recognize that many adopted people also worry their search will be hurtful or unwelcome by their family of experience. It takes strength for the adoptive family to put aside their fears and stand in support of their loved one. As supporters, it is so critical to acknowledge that the adopted person is seeking vital information, information that non adopted people often take for granted. Being able to access our full history should be a primal human right, regardless of whether or not a person uses the information to facilitate reunions. Having been denied this basic right for so long impacts the adopted person in many ways, often making it difficult for your loved one to truly believe they are deserving. Your role is to continue to validate this basic right and provide what the adopted person needs on this emotional journey, not what you may need to assuage your own fears and worries. It may be useful to reach out for your own support to work through these difficulties in order to limit them interfering with your ability to provide unbiased support for your loved one.

The richest journeys in our lives rarely come with clear outcomes at the beginning and often have no concrete end point. Rather, these are journeys that continuously evolve, and it is in the process of the experience that true growth occurs.

REFERENCE

Evan B. Donaldson Adoption Institute (2009). *Beyond Culture Camp: Promoting healthy identity formation in adoption.* Retrieved from: http://adoptioninstitute.org/old/publications/2009_11_BeyondCultureCamp.pdf

The Search Process: Roadblocks and Creative Solutions

Wendy Barkett

Wendy was born in 1972 and raised in a closed adoption in Ohio. She began her search for truth at the age of eighteen and found some of her answers forteen-years-later in 2004. She continues to write from the heart without any filters in hopes of bringing a better understanding to those who decide to join her journey. As the first Ohio adoptee to receive her original birth certificate on March 20th, 2015, she continues to speak of her search as well as the feelings surrounding it with hopes that all states will open their records to adoptees.

* * *

In writing this chapter it is my hope that at some point the need for any tips or thoughts on an adoptee searching will soon be a moot point. I had grown up with the full knowledge that I had been adopted. The story in my family was that my parents were only seemingly able to produce boys and my father wanted a daughter. My parents hired an attorney, and when a female child finally arrived, they came and got me bringing along their two biological sons, my older brothers. The story of my family bringing me home is a comforting story, and I would on occasion ask my mother to tell me the story again. There was never any doubt that I was loved and adored. I knew though that in order for my parents to be able to choose me, I had another set of parents that made the choice not to keep me. I knew that I had to find them and hopefully find out more about them.

There has not ever been a time in my life where I had to question if I would search for birth family or not. I always knew that this was a need for myself. In my early teen years I decided that on my 18th birthday I would request my adoption file from the Probate Court in the city my adoption was facilitated. What I did not know was that because my state was a closed records state, I would be denied my file. On my 18th birthday I took the two and a half hour drive with much anticipation of what might be in that file. I was nervous and excited at the same time and had my ID in hand as I approached the Clerk. When I said "I'm here to get my adoption file" she replied with a laugh and said, "That's not how it works." I was sent away feeling a frustration that was beyond description.

My search began in 1990. This was well before the personal computer or internet. This was a time of personal struggle and growth for myself, this was also when I left the state I had been born, adopted, and raised in. While my parents had shared with me a few details about my birth parents they had very little they could tell me as anything they had destroyed anything they had received per the advice of their attorney. I knew the height and weight as well as the age of my birth parents, and that was all. My first attempt at searching was by mail. I sent a letter to the pediatrician who had tended to me for so many years and asked him for my medical files. I explained that as a wife to a man in the military, it would be best to mail the records directly to me as I never knew which doctor I might be seeing. A few weeks later I received my medical file in the form of a letter. I looked at that letter for some time and was able to make out some truths I had already known: my birth mother's age, as well as, the fact that I was born early. I also found out a private issue my birth mother may have had and could not help but to notice the large capital "A" (Adopted) circled at the top of my file.

This medical file is what began to fuel my need to search more. My next step was in 1992 to contact Adoption Network Cleveland. I did not know if it was a group that could help me or not, but I felt like I needed to find out more information from them as they were still in Ohio while I resided in Texas. I was sent a wealth of information as well as a better understanding of the law and their continued efforts to change the law in Ohio. It was overwhelming, and I still felt at a loss in my search. The letter they sent me in reply was tucked away with my medical records.

My husband and I purchased a computer; the internet or world wide web was now in existence! I did not understand what it meant, but as we played with this new thing called the internet I was amazed at how much information was now at my fingertips! Now my search began to charge full steam ahead. I looked up Ohio adoption law and came across an interesting page which offered a form that I could fill out, have notarized, and mail in to the Probate Court, and with a small fee, I would receive my "Non Identifying Information." In April of 2000, my letter from the Court arrived. It felt like a very thin envelope, and having no idea what to expect I opened it with some hesitation as well as anticipation.

Re: Release of Non-Identifying Information

This single page release offered me ten new facts. One line on the release "School grade completed" for both birth parents was left blank. However, I finally was able to add a fact to the story of my adoption that I had only been able to make up along the way - my birth mother was married, my birth father however was not. This was a huge answer in one of my standard questions of why was I placed for adoption. Now I knew. Now I began to stand a little bit taller.

The cover letter included with my non identifying information stated in part "If the petitioner was adopted but there are no releases on file and the agency or Court does not determine that the biological parents are deceased, the Judge shall order the Petition to remain pending until withdrawn by the petitioner or there are subsequent filings of release or until the death of the biological parents." I filled out the petition that they had sent to me, filled out a check, mailed it back to Ohio, and then I waited.

I called my parents to share with them the new information I had received in the mail. I had not often spoken of my adoption with my parents as it always felt to me like it was not a very welcomed subject, at least not any of my questions about where I had come from or how I had come to be an adoptee. As they were and are my parents, I felt the need to share with them some of the information that I had though like the fact that I was born a different religion then I had been raised. When I told them this my mother's reply was, "Well of course we knew that." I asked her why they had never told me of this information, and she replied that she never felt there was any reason to. I did not have the words at that time to explain that while it did not seem important or significant to them, it actually helped me to feel a little bit more whole. The fact remained, though, that they knew this information, and while they could not reverse time to change what they had or had not told me, I felt lied to and lost some trust in them.

In October of 2000, I received a reply to my petition which stated that there "does contain a release of identity information filed by biological sibling of petitioner." I also received a letter with my Order that stated that "the agency has filed a report that no releases have been filed by your birth parents at the Ohio Bureau of Vital Statistics." It all became very confusing for me. I continued to search online. I also reached back out to the Court and asked that they notify my birth parents that I was looking for them. I received a letter informing me that this was not something the Court would do. I wrote the Governor, I wrote the hospital which I had been born in and stayed for five days, and I continued to search online.

In 2002, I again requested information from the Court
and received an Amended Order which stated that my file
did not have a release from any birth parent or sibling.
This Amended Order had my own name incorrect on it,
so they sent yet a second Amended Order. Dealing with
the Court, with what may have felt like simple mistakes
on their end, was emotionally draining. I had found an
online group of adoptees where you could post threads
and share your story as well as support others. I felt it
was a safe place to vent my feelings, and I learned that
many of the feelings I had were rather common to other
adoptees.

Talk shows of the late 1990's and early 2000's continued
to play hour-long programs where birth family would
reunite on television. I wrote each and every show and
pleaded for them to help me. In searching online, I found
many sites that offered assistance to adoptees or birth
family searching, some required a fee, others were free. I
could not figure out why no matter how many sites I
posted my information on no one seemed to be looking
for me. My best guess was that my birth mother either did
not have access to a computer or did not know about the
same sites I knew about. I did my best not to get
discouraged while also helping others in their own
search.

In 2004, I listed a painting on Ebay. It was a purple
dachshund with a rhinestone collar. At the bottom of my
listing I explained that any proceeds made from the sale
of the painting would go towards my adoption search. I
was at a point where I felt I was going to try and hire
someone to do my search for me as I felt I had run out of
options. The woman who purchased my painting sent me

an email explaining that the painting was purchased for her daughter who was adopted. This adoptive mother told me that if and when her daughter decided to search for her own biological family she would assist her in all possible ways. I was blown away by the support she would someday offer her daughter. Another person saw my purple dachshund listing and sent me a message. She told me of a woman to contact who assisted in searching locally in Ohio. She lived about forty minutes from the Court where my files remained. I sent this woman an email and she replied quickly.

There was a small fee; she explained that this fee would cover gas, parking meters, and other expenses. If she did not use the entire fee, it would be passed on to the next person's search for it was a basic rate and all searches could take more or less time requiring more or less gas and parking fees. I agreed and sent her a check as well as all of the information I had so far. She kept me posted by phone or email as to what steps they were taking. When she told me they were headed to Vital Statistics to search the birth records on micro film I did not understand what it meant but waited for my next update.

On June 7th of 2004, I received an email from my searcher which asked that I call her as soon as possible. June 7th is 5 days after my birthday, it is my mother's birthday, and it is also the date I was brought home by my adoptive parents. I called my searcher, and she told me they had my birth mother's name. They needed to locate her, and it should not take much time since the spelling of her first name was rather unique. I sat down that evening and wrote a letter to my birth mother. I wanted to share with her a little about myself and hoped she would receive it well. I finished the letter and then proceeded to throw it in the trash. Something did not feel right.

The following morning I again had an email from my searcher asking that I call her, and so I once again did. This time she had to share the horrible news with me - my birth mother had died. It was not recent; my birth mother had died 13 months after my birth in the very city where I was born and adopted. It was in the newspapers, and so she had already placed a copy in an envelope to mail to me. I wanted to believe this was all a mistake. I had in that moment not only lost my biological mother; I had also lost all of the dreams I had of meeting her, seeing her, or talking to her. I had lost 32 years of wishes.

Per my birth mother's obituary my searcher informed me that I had a sibling, an older sister, and they would next work on finding her. As a result of their hard work, I had my sister's name and phone number the next day. It was a Friday, and I spoke with her that evening for a couple of hours. She did not know of my existence but welcomed me without hesitation. I spoke to my sister for the first time on July 16, 2004. I feel it is of no coincidence that the anniversary of her mother, of my biological mother's death was July 17, 1973. My sister lost her mother before the age of six, and some thirty-two-years later, I called to say hello.

My sister gave me as much information as she could about Dottye, her mother and my birth mother. She sent me photos through email, and we spoke often on the phone but more often by way of email. What she could not share with me though was who my birth father was. While her own father was deceased, he had lived until my sister married with her own children, and yet he never told her about my existence. I will never really be able to understand that. I spoke to his widow (he remarried after Dottye died) and she told me that she knew that Dottye had been pregnant, but that he had always said that I ended up being miscarried.

I called my parents after speaking to my sister the first time. I made sure they were both on the phone as I shared with them that my birth mother had died and had in fact been dead since 1973. I also told them that I located a sister and had reason to believe that there might be other siblings. My parents did their best to be supportive in their own words, though I learned from that conversation to filter my information to them. There was a fine line between giving them facts and feeling like I was hurting their feelings or betraying them, and I learned to walk that line during that conversation.

In all of my years of searching and wondering, I always thought that once I found my birth mother the rest of my search would fall into place. I thought that I would find her, ask her who my birth father was, and that would be the end of my questions. It had not occurred to me that I would find my birth mother at a grave. I thought I had begun my search early enough that age would not have taken her yet. I was right; age did not take her, a car accident did. She was twenty-four-years old at the time of her death. The man she had been unfaithful to but remained married to was now deceased, and my only thought was that I needed to find people who knew Dottye in order to finish my search.

In 2004, I sent the Court a death certificate for Dottye, and they in turn sent me more information from my adoption file. I continued to share this information with my sister as I felt it had some impact on her life as well. The document was called "Placement Report" and shared a little information about Dottye's feelings at the time she was still pregnant with me, as well as information on her own family. I had in writing that she too had been adopted, and I knew upon reading that, that at some point I would need to research her roots. This document also verified that Dottye had two more children prior to myself and my older sister who had been placed for adoption at birth when she was in high school. The record offered the year they were born but not much else. This document also offered a little more information on my birth father though it did not offer me his name.

I decided I would next try and locate the other siblings. I felt like I needed to let them know that Dottye was dead. I worried that they too might be wondering why she never looked for them. I searched the internet to try and find these adopted siblings to no avail. I hired a Confidential Intermediary (CI) in the state my siblings had been born and adopted in to try and locate either of them. She located one, but he did not want any contact. What was interesting is the year that was in my placement record for this person's birth and the year this person was actually born were off by one year.I asked her if there was another child placed for adoption in their file as there should have been one more adoptee, being older then the one she found. She said there was not any mention of this other adoptee in the file.

I knew that Dottye had another child who was older, so I knew I still had to look. I decided to try contacting people Dottye would have gone to high school with and joined the group online called classmates. I joined classmates using Dottye's name and the year we thought she may have graduated at her high school. The site had a limit to how many emails could be sent out each day, and each day I met that limit. I introduced myself to those I sent emails to as Dottye's daughter. I explained that she had passed away in 1973 in a car accident, and that I was looking for anyone who remembered her in hopes that they would share their memories.

I ended up finding very few people who knew her. In total about three people actually knew her and shared their memories of her or the time they spent with her. I cherished these shared memories as I now knew I would never have any of my own. I also found a person who did not know Dottye personally, but he knew the man who had fathered her first child. I found out that like her other child, the year was written in my placement record was actually a year off from the actual birth. I found this person and once again found a sibling who did not want to have any contact. While it was painful and it felt like I was being rejected, I learned that it was nearly impossible to actually have been rejected. The two siblings who decided they did not want contact did not know me, so any rejection was based on the idea, not on me personally. Even without contact I felt that I had done what I set out to do. I sent them both letters as well as photos and explained who their birth parents were as well as as the fact that Dottye had died in 1973. It was time to again focus my attention on finding out who my birth father was. It was time to think outside of the box.

My sister had told me once when we first were speaking to each other that she thought she knew who my father was. She said his name "Waylon Jennings" and I had to ask "Who is that?". My sister was raised with a story about how her father got into a fist fight with Waylon Jennings in a club, a fight presumably over Dottye. I am not one to listen to country music, but he was not hard to find on the computer; a simple search of his name brought up tons of images and pages of information. I learned that here in Texas, in a city called Littlefield, there is a Waylon Jennings museum. My husband and I decided to take a flight to a town nearby and drive on over to the museum. We walked through the small but packed room after being greeted by the cashier with a warm welcome and friendly smile. I stood looking at all of the items with his signature and then saw some large family photos on the wall. I stood before the largest of the photos and could not help but to wonder *are these people family? Are these all half siblings???*

It was about that time that the friendly clerk approached us. With tears in my eyes I explained to her my mission to find my birth father, knowing full well I likely sounded like I was a tad crazy. It was then that I found out that Waylon was her Uncle. I showed her Dottye's photos and she said maybe I should show them to her dad, Waylon's brother. He had just stopped by and so I did just that. I told him I had reason to believe he and Dottye knew each other. When he looked at the photos he said "Well ya, she'd be someone Waylon would have liked." Waylon's niece did not think her father would have anything to do with DNA testing so we left that day once again feeling exhausted and drained and with more questions then answers.

A week went by, then I got a letter in the mail from her and she said she had an Uncle, another of Waylon's brothers, who was willing to do the DNA test with us. It was near Thanksgiving time when my husband and I took the 10 hour round trip drive to Littlefield to do our DNA test together with this brother of Waylon Jennings. It was a long drive there and an exhausting drive back home as it had snowed (and those of you who are living in the South know that southerners do not deal well with snow). While at her house we spoke about Dottye and about my search. It was then that Waylon's brother shared with us that Dottye once ran Waylon's fan club, while she was still a teen in Arizona. When Waylon's family needed to know where Waylon was, they would contact her. She knew all of his shows and ran a great fan club; this was back in the 1960's. We also found out that Waylon had also done shows in Las Vegas. I felt like anything I had thought I had learned about my birth father was likely a lie to try and cover up who he really was. We finished about an hour's worth of visiting and drove back home with our DNA in envelopes ready to be mailed the next day. In less than a month's time I got the email letting me know that I could use my special log in number to see my results. I was devastated when I saw that we were not a match at all, meaning that Waylon was not my father.

I decided to again focus on the information from those placement records that my father was part Italian, born in Boston and met my mother Dottye when she had gone to Las Vegas. He worked there, she stated as a Keno Writer. I took a trip to Las Vegas for a five day research visit. I went to the University where I spent one day photo copying the entire 1970 Con Directory, a criss cross directory similar to a phone book but offered more information including what type of work as well as where the head of household was employed. This was a long task and worth the time in many ways. I would research that directory when I got home. I also went to a local library where I scanned some micro film in hopes of finding some sort of classified ad telling my father that I was being placed for adoption - also a time consuming task. While I did not find any such ads for myself I did for other families, so I know it was at least done some of the time.

I went into every casino that was still open and had existed in 1971. I would ask for anyone who might have worked there in the 1970's, my hope was to find someone who would reply "Oh, I did, and yes, I remember Dottye" but that never happened. I did meet a lot of nice people though who kept me energized with their stories of back in the day. By this time I had started a website about my search and made sure to hand a business card to anyone who would take it. This trip was draining and took me well out of my comfort level, so while I did not find my birth father, I chalked it up to part of my life journey.

When I got home from the trip I began to read and research the Con Directory. I scanned over a thousand pages and highlighted anyone who was a Keno Writer or any job along those lines. It was a long shot; what I really needed was a Con Directory from 1972 to have a more accurate list of who was in the area in 1971 (the time of my conception) but I went with what I had. For each person I found in the Keno line of work, I researched and looked up current addresses for them and began mailing out letters. Each letter included a SASE as well as photos of Dottye. In all, I mailed out over 200 letters. Many came back marked return to sender. I got some replies simply stating that they did not know her, but one man called and had an interesting story. His father was deceased but spoke of Dottye often and with much admiration. He was playing Keno one night and was not playing well at all. Dottye approached him and taught him how to play the game, and he later won a large amount of money. She also helped him to get home one evening when he was too drunk to make it on his own. Given this story with such admiration the man who called me, agreed to take a DNA test with me so we could find out if his now deceased father was also mine. By this time my sister and I had done several large online DNA tests to a) verify that we were half sisters and b) try and figure out who my father was per matching other people in the DNA database for each company. I decided to test this man at one of the companies I had already tested with so that if we did not match, he could still have fun learning more about other people who matched him. When the results came back, we found out we were not a match. I will forever be grateful to him for sharing the stories with me though.

My husband and I took a trip to Las Vegas, meeting my sister and her husband there. I had contacted three major networks to see if any of them would be willing to air a story about my search. I continued to email them until the day we left for our trip, and Fox 5 was the only station to show interest and follow through with filming a story. It aired several times that night and was much longer then I had thought it would be. It was great coverage but did not produce any results. However, I was once again able to say that I had made a goal and reached it.

With few ideas left on how to find out who my birth father was, I continued to check my DNA results weekly at the three companies I had tested with. I tested my half-sister at two of the companies as well, so I was able to narrow down the maternal versus paternal matches to some degree. The three companies I tested at were: Ancestry, 23andme, and Familytreedna. I took the raw data provided from Ancestry and loaded it to a site called GedMatch. GedMatch is a free site with many tools offered, my main concern was looking for closely related matches. Each company has a different way of displaying results as well as different tools and prices. I have read for years now about many people being able to figure out who their birth families are using the DNA sites. Through Ancestry I was able to able to make some connections to my maternal side and found out who Dottye's birth family was. I have been able to work her tree back to the 1800's which was a pretty amazing task to accomplish! While her birth parents are both deceased I was able to obtain photos of them through other family members, again found on Ancestry.

The search for my birth father had come to a lull. I continued to check my DNA results daily and had been informed by an expert in DNA Genealogy that it could take years to figure out who he is because his parents or grandparents were direct immigrants to the United States, and not many of my matches appear to be in the paternal line. Actually, less than one-percent of my matches are from my paternal side, and they are so distant that there is not a way to make a connection. My case is very non typical though, and I highly recommend doing a DNA test to find out not only who your relatives are but also to get a look at your heritage. I loved finding out that I am in fact part Italian, knowing full well that this part of my heritage came from my birth father.

It was at the end of the month, March 2016, when I did my daily ritual. With a cup of coffee in hand I checked my DNA. I began with Ancestry and felt my hands begin to shake as I saw the new match. A first cousin once removed! He had no "Relatives in common" and that is how I knew he was a cousin from my paternal side. He did not have anyone listed in his family tree beyond his grandparents. I reached out to the group on FaceBook called DNA Detectives as I had in the past and then the real excitement began. I was lucky enough to be attending an adoption conference in Ohio, Adoption Network Cleveland Annual Adoption Gathering, and Amanda, from DNA Detectives, was teaching a class on DNA. Amanda and I knew each other online and she knew my story. That evening she took me aside and sat with me for a couple of hours as we searched the internet as well as Ancestry, trying to piece together who this new cousin of mine was. We determined that my next step would be to reach out to him via the messaging program at Ancestry. When I took a day to regather from my conference weekend I sent him a simple message. I was more nervous then I had ever been about making contact as this felt like my only link, and likely was my only link, to finding out who my birth father was. When I did not hear back from him, Amanda was kind enough to make contact. She played the middle person for some time and was finally able to get him on the phone. She was able to explain to him how DNA works as well as explain in more detail who I am. He had done the test to learn more about his heritage and was not aware that he would be matched up to relatives. The way she spoke to him helped him to not only better understand how DNA works, but also understand my search. While Amanda worked as the middle person I continued to work on my tree, though at the time it was my cousins tree. I was working up both sides of his tree in order to find a man in it who might match my non identifying information. I felt like I was still hitting dead ends as no one was fitting my non identifying information (this often happens) then he made mention to Amanda about an Uncle who had already passed away.

We figured out through the DNA tools that this first cousin match was a first cousin once removed, meaning that his mother was actually my direct first cousin. I began a new tree, this time I was the main person. I built the tree up and out, including my first cousin and her parents, then grandparents. I researched the name given to us, of the deceased Uncle, and we found that while there was not much information about him online, there was enough to fill in the gaps. We had finally, after just shy of 26 years, finished my search.

Unlike my search for Dottye I had some idea that I might very well find a grave at the end of this search as I knew the person who was my birth father had been born in 1942, and so he would be around the age of 74. It was still heartbreaking though, and I continue to try and work through those feelings. He actually died just shy of his 55th birthday. I ordered a copy of his death certificate and am now able to share at least part of his medical history with my own doctor. I have also requested his military records and at this time am still waiting to receive those.

When I shared the news with my parents I again knew I had to be gentle with the way I presented this information to them. Gentle in order to protect myself as well as them. My feelings had been so hurt over some of the things they had said in the past that it surprised me when my feelings were once again hurt at their reaction to the news. I do not however regret sharing with them as it is my nature to be honest, though holding back some of the details is something I continue to do.

The one thing I felt I needed to feel like my search was complete was a photo of my birth father, Michael. I did find two photos of him on Ancestry however they did not satisfy my need because they were from when he was in high school, very grainy, and did not give me an idea of who he was as an adult. I continued to search with the help of two people online and was able to obtain a mailing address for a woman that Michael had been married and divorced from before my birth. I sent her a letter, or shall we call it a plea, explaining to her who I was gently and requesting contact with her. In this letter (and in any letters that I mail out to possible contacts) I included my phone number, my mailing address as well as my email address. The day that she received my letter, she sent me an email. She has been open and honest to the core, and I have thanked her more then once for showing me the respect of her honesty. She no longer had any photos of him which did not surprise me since they were after all divorced so long ago, but she was able to answer some basic questions as well as offer her support. One morning she sent me an email with a name: the best man at their wedding. She had also told me the name of a cousin that Mike had been close to, but unfortunately the cousin had passed away three years ago. The best man however was still living. I sent him a message via FaceBook and saw that he read it, however he did not reply. I decided then to send him a land letter in hopes that by seeing my handwriting the realness of me as a person would come through. It worked! He sent me a message via FaceBook the day after he received my letter and said that he had indeed seen my message but thought it was some sort of spam. Over the past couple of weeks he has shared with me things as he remembers them. He was best friends with Michael but they lost contact about 15 years before Michael died. Michael's mother did however call this best friend to tell him of his passing.

The priceless gift I got from this best friend was a photo. It dates back to the 1980's which is ten years plus after my birth. It is perfect. It is aged, it is a photo of Micheal sitting on the couch with his best friend, and it is not posed. It is a priceless gift. Had I not continued to reach out I might never have seen what Michael looked like as an adult.

When I announced on social media (after emailing and or speaking to my family) that I had found my birth father, and then shared his photo, I was a tad surprised at the reactions. People were overwhelmingly happy for me, for many of them have followed my search for many years. What surprised me was the number of people who asked, without a moment, how did he die? I needed time to absorb the reality of his death, as well as the way he died. It pained me for people to want to know the full story so quickly. What I needed time to realize is to them this is a story. It is a story I have offered openly, and they were ready to read the last page. For myself the last page was a long time coming, and I was not ready yet to close the book. When I shared the photo of Michael, myself in the middle, and Dottye, the reaction was amazing. It helped to close the chapter of who I came from, not just one side, but both sides.

I have been asked if I regret my search, I think often times this question is asked because of the length of time that my search took. I also think people ask because when you are open on social media sometimes people forget that while my search was intense and rather time consuming, I do have a life outside of search. Though the search—or my adoption, are forever in my mind, I do enjoy other activities. My answer is without a doubt no. No, I do not regret my search. I am sad that I never got to meet either of my birth parents, I am sorry that the laws adding length to time used in my search, but I do not regret my search. I stand taller, I can now look in the mirror without feeling like I am a soulless shell, and I have met some amazing people along the way. Search is not for everyone, but for myself there was never any doubt that I had to do the search completely to the end. I had to find the two people who brought me into this world.

In closing, I would like to mention two things. One is to be open to helping others. I obtained my Original Birth Certificate "OBC" in 2004 after sending the courts Dottye's death certificate. This document did not give me any new information, but I felt a little more whole having it. The law in Ohio however did not allow other adoptees to have theirs. So, when I had the chance to help, I did. Adoption Network Cleveland shared with me a law they were working on to open the records. I spoke before the Senate to share my story with them. I had flown in to tell them how I felt changing the law was important. In March of 2014, the new law went into effect, allowing all Ohio adoptees the right to have their OBC. I was also honored to be the first of five adoptees to receive my OBC during the opening ceremony. This new law had no effect on my own search but I still worked towards seeing it changed in hopes that others will now feel that searching is their choice, as well as the knowledge that they can have their OBC even if they do not want to search.

The second thing I would like to address is also a very personal opinion. Searching should be up to the adoptee. I know for myself I often felt like I had no say in my adoption, I wanted to have the only say in my search. No one should ever be pushed into searching for birth family; it is a very personal choice. On that same note, no one should ever be pushed out of searching for their birth family. There should be no guilt and no question as to why an adoptee wants to search or doesn't want to. My search had nothing to do with my family. They are still my family. I do not love them any less. I still need them as much as I did before my search. My search was about my own need to find out where my roots were from, it was a part of my own personal growth.

Why I Am Not Searching

Christina Romo

Christina Romo was adopted from South Korea at age two. She works for an adoption organization and shares her journey as an adoptee through her blog, *Diary of a Not-So-Angry Asian Adoptee*. Her writing has also been featured in The Huffington Post, The Good Men Project, and BlogHer. She lives in Minnesota with her husband and their two sons.

* * *

I have a DNA testing kit. I requested it almost a year ago, thinking it would take a while to receive as there had been a waiting list and a seemingly short supply of available kits. Much to my surprise, it arrived within a week of my request, and it has been sitting on a shelf ever since. The kit is still in the original mailing envelope—untouched and collecting dust.

There are tens of thousands of people adopted from Korea who are living in the United States, and I happen to be one of them. I was born in the early 1980's, when the relinquishment of children in Korea seemed somewhat commonplace. It is almost as though the country had become desensitized to the daily discovery of children who were abandoned on the side of the road or on the steps of orphanages and police stations. Family is everything in Korea, and I was born at a time when it was extremely rare for families to adopt children with whom they did not share a bloodline. Adoptions were often performed in secret, and many children who were adopted domestically were never told they were adopted. There was also a great stigma placed on unwed mothers. Many found themselves without the means or support to raise a child on their own and had no choice but to relinquish their children and hope they would be well cared for and loved by families who could provide for them and give them a good life.

I was found in a subway station in Seoul, South Korea, when I was a year old. The few sentences provided to my parents about the circumstances in which I was found stated that I was crying and had bruising around my eyes. I was left without a name, a birthdate, or any clues as to my birth family's identity or why I was abandoned. In hindsight, I believe having the knowledge of *something*— an indication that I was *somebody* to *someone*—may have made my abandonment a little less painful. The relinquishment of a child was seemingly treated in a very "just the facts" manner in Korea, and there was very little thought or care given to what that would truly mean for the child. Some mothers left their children with trinkets or letters so their child would know they were loved and with the hope that these little clues would one day help them to reconnect with their children. There is a chance that I may have been left with something, but like countless other adoptees, those seemingly meaningless objects that may have actually meant the world to us were tossed aside and never shared with us or with the families who adopted us.

I spent a year in Korea before I was adopted. During that year, I was given a name—Soon Duk Kim—and assigned a date of birth. I remember nothing of that time, but I have experienced dreams in which I have visions and flashes of shadowy figures standing over me as I laid in a crib. I have no way of knowing whether or not these visions are actual memories or simply fantasies I concocted in my mind at some point during my adoption journey. The visions are always very stark and cold, with no feelings of warmth or love. As with many children who were relinquished, I suspect I suffered a great deal of neglect during that time between my relinquishment and my adoption. At times, I find myself intensely afraid of the dark and of being left alone—both of which I believe stem from my experiences during my first two years of life.

I came to America and met my family for the first time on the same day I presumably turned two years old. My dad is a first-generation American—his family emigrated from Italy before settling in New York. My mom was born and raised in Minnesota and is of primarily German-descent. My parents met on a blind date while attending separate colleges and married in Minnesota before moving to D.C. where my dad served in the Army, working at the Pentagon, and my mom worked as an environmental health specialist. They eventually moved back and planted their roots in Minnesota before adopting my sister from Korea in 1982. I was adopted in 1984, and my parents gave birth to my brother a year later.

My parents adopted my sister and me at a time when very little was known about adoption issues. They were given very little information and were essentially told to take us home and love us and everything would be okay. My parents did really well with what little information they were given. While we did not necessarily talk about adoption, the fact that my sister and I were adopted was never hidden from us—which would have been difficult for them to do anyway, considering the fact that we were a mixed race family. My parents honored and embraced our Korean culture in a number of wonderful ways. When choosing names for us, my parents ensured that we would always have a part of our heritage by keeping our Korean surnames as our middle names. They sent my sister and me to Korean culture camp for a week each summer for a number of years, gave us hanboks (the traditional Korean dress), and learned how to make Korean food. The information my parents had about our lives in Korea was put into scrapbooks for us to read when we were ready to do so. I believe my mom was actually a little ahead of her time in putting the scrapbooks together for us, as they included much of the same information included in today's Life Books.

My family lived in a predominantly Caucasian neighborhood, and my siblings and I attended a private school where my sister and I were a part of a very small percentage of non-Caucasian students. My brother and sister were both popular, good-looking, and fit in well. I was an awkward, shy, and hypersensitive kid—a combination that often did not fare well during my younger years. I was different. I had a very different background than the other kids, and I was well aware and very sensitive to how different I truly was.

On the surface, I had a really good childhood. I grew up in a middle-class family where we always had clothes on our backs and food on the table. My parents were always very loving and supportive, and worked hard to provide us with many wonderful opportunities. My parents encouraged and supported us in the pursuit of our goals and interests, instilled in us values that we carry with us and have passed on to our children, and always made sure we knew that we were loved and cherished.

I have always been a somewhat neurotic and self-deprecating person who internalizes everything. This made for a really tough combination as a child. Though I was a very awkward and hypersensitive kid, I seemed well adjusted in the sense that I had friends and did well in school. On the inside, I was hurting and really struggling with issues related to my adoption. Regardless of how much my parents loved me and how often they told me so, I often feared making a mistake or doing something that would make my parents want to send me back to Korea. That fear of abandonment developed into a perfectionist child mentality. I worked hard to be a good daughter, and I worked hard to excel academically. I wanted so badly to be the daughter I believed my parents wanted and often sacrificed who I was in the process of trying to do what I thought would please them and make them happy. I had convinced myself that if I was good enough—if I tried hard enough—they would not have a reason to abandon me. My parents did nothing to cause me to feel this way, but as a result of the loss of my birth family, my brain had been wired to believe from a very young age that people who love you will leave you. The overwhelming fear of abandonment and the need to protect my heart from further rejection became an integral part of my childhood and teen years.

I rarely talked about how I was feeling or shared my fears with anyone when I was younger, and I still can sometimes feel the effects of carrying that pain, anger, grief, and anxiety around with me for so long. It breaks my heart to think how loved I was as a child and how I rarely allowed myself to feel worthy of that love. In many ways, I was a child who felt so much yet understood so little.

As an adult, I realize how irrational my fears were as a child, but they were very real to me while growing up. There were nights when I wished on every star I could see and prayed for God to let me look like all of the other girls. I hated my dark hair and my Asian eyes and thought that if I could look like everyone else on the outside that I might actually feel on the inside like I belonged. Like some adoptees, I fantasized about my life and my family in Korea. There were some nights where I dreamed of my birth mother, and I imagined her telling me that she loved me. But, many nights were spent mourning the loss of my birth mother, questioning why she did not love me enough to keep me, and hating her for throwing me away as though I was nothing more than a piece of garbage.

I remember a teacher in middle school who decided to incorporate adoption into his lesson for the day. I will never forget how it felt as he looked straight at me and began his lesson with the words—*"You were adopted because your birth mother didn't want you."* It happened over two decades ago, but the words still sting as though I had heard them yesterday. While it was incredibly humiliating and heartbreaking to have that happen in front of my classmates, it bothered me more to hear someone else verbalize something I had secretly felt for years. The most difficult part for me was that I did not know the truth. I could not tell him that he was wrong, because a part of me feared that he was right.

There were times in my life where I was very proud of being Korean and other times where I rejected that part of who I was in an effort to fit in. When I was younger, I used to have very real and very irrational fears about going back to Korea. I had nightmares about being forced to go back and not being able to leave. While I yearned to fit in and not look so different as a little girl, I was also terrified of becoming lost in a sea of people who looked just like me. Throughout my adoption journey, I have been asked on numerous occasions whether or not I would want to go back to Korea and if I would ever want to search for my birth family. The question itself is often a stark reminder of the fact that I do not truly belong anywhere. I will never feel like I completely belong in America, and because I do not have a connection to the language or culture, I would not have a prayer of belonging in Korea either.

In a strange way, I have found great comfort in the belief that there is nothing for me in Korea. Rather than searching the countless crowds for a face that looks even a little like my own, I have found that it is easier to not wonder—to not hope for someone whom I was never meant to find. Adoption is so complex in so many ways, and I often feel as though I am wandering aimlessly through and caught somewhere in between. I would like to return to Korea with my husband and sons someday so we can learn about and experience some of the culture together, but I do not plan to search at all while there. That journey back to Korea will not happen anytime soon as I still experience a great amount of anxiety just thinking about it; a small part of me still has difficulties letting go of that ridiculously irrational fear I had as a child of not being able to leave if I were to ever go back.

I have a lot of mixed feelings about my birth mother that change often. There are days when I really miss her, which often feels strange to me, considering the fact that I do not know her at all. There are days when I feel an overwhelming amount of hate and anger towards her. There are days when I feel empathy for her and the decision she made to let me go. There are days when I imagine meeting her, and I am overwhelmed at the thought of meeting a complete stranger who will always have a piece of my heart…a complete stranger who made a series of decisions that have affected the entire trajectory of my life. What would it feel like to meet someone for whom you have spent your entire life mourning? How do you say hello to someone who never gave you the chance to say goodbye?

When I think about wanting to search for my birth family, I find myself struggling with the fear of the unknown and the fear of knowing. Based on the information provided, it is clear that there was a history of abuse and, presumably, neglect in my birth family. To what extent, I will never know, but the facts are as clear as the words on the piece of paper I have read countless times throughout my life. As with many people with traumatic histories, the fear of the self-fulfilling prophecy and history repeating itself is very real and can be very overwhelming. If I experienced abuse, does that mean that I could become an abusive person? My birth mother was not able to parent me, so does that mean that I will not be a good parent to my children? If someone in my birth family caused me harm, how could I possibly want anything to do with them?

I don't think I will ever be in a place where I will be okay with committing myself fully to search for my birth family. There is too much pain, too much anger, too much confusion. There are too many questions—some of which I could never bring myself to ask, and some for which I would never want to know the answers. There will always be a part of me that truly believes that my birth mother does not want to be found. I often fear that the reality of the situation and the circumstances that lead to my relinquishment will be too much for me to ever be able to process and too painful for my heart to bear. While I have heard a number of wonderful reunification stories, I have also heard many stories of rejection, heartbreaking discoveries, and searches that only lead to more questions that will never be answered.

I often describe my life as a puzzle with many missing pieces. In a strange way, I find it comforting to believe that my puzzle was never meant to be complete. An unfinished symphony can still be beautiful and meaningful, and I feel the same way about my life. I do not want to hope for the continuation of a chapter that never really had a beginning. Hope can be so beautiful, but it can be incredibly heartbreaking and soul shattering as well. I do not want to spend my life searching every crowd for a face that looks like mine. I do not want to chase after a dream that was never meant to be. I want to believe that my birth mother is at peace with her decision and has lived a good life since she closed the chapter on the life she shared with me.

My sons are old enough to understand in their own way what it means for them to have a parent who was adopted. My younger son is more intrigued by the fact that I was adopted and often struggles to comprehend why my birth parents were not able to keep me. I have found that he often comes to his own conclusion that they must have been sick or are no longer alive. I do share with him that there is a strong possibility that my birth parents are still alive, but I ultimately allow him to believe whatever brings him the most comfort. At some point, I do plan to actually complete the DNA test to learn about my birth family's medical history. Knowing that piece of the puzzle will be important for my children and may help provide some clarity with regard to some of my own health issues. I feel a responsibility as their mom to at least attempt to answer some of those questions for my sons and for the children I hope they will someday bring into the world. However, I do not plan to opt into the relative search.

My birth mother brought me into this world, and she presumably cared for me for a year prior to my relinquishment. I will never minimize the sacrifice she made, and though her decision sometimes makes me feel as though I was unwanted, I choose to believe that she walked away from me that day with love in her heart and hope for the dreams she had for me. I will never know if she thinks about me or wonders about the person I have become. I will never be grateful for the decision my birth mother made that led to the loss of the connections to my birth family, my culture, and my country of origin. It hurts to mourn the loss of a complete stranger who made the decision not to know me all those years ago. I will never truly know if she wanted me to find her or if I was wanted or loved. There will always be a part of me that will wonder, but I have found peace with my decision to not search for my birth family. Though I will never know who in my birth family shares my smile, my love of music, or my passion for writing, I am okay with not knowing. I am okay with loving my birth mother without knowing her.

I have lived a good life. My parents provided me with the unconditional love, support, guidance, encouragement, and opportunities that have helped me to become the person I am today. They held my hands and helped me face the storms during the darkest times in my life, and they were there to pick me up when I hit rock bottom. I have made decisions in my life that I am not proud of, and there were times when I caused myself and my parents a great deal of pain. They never gave up, and they fought hard to stay by my side, regardless of how hard I tried to push them away. I have often questioned my worth and whether I deserve to be loved, but it has never been a question for them. It did not matter that the faces in the crowd during my basketball games, school musicals, recitals, choir concerts, and my high school and college graduations did not look like me. The faces I searched for in the crowd were those of my family who loved and supported me unconditionally, and that mattered to me more than anything. My parents were there to walk me down the aisle on my wedding day, and they have been a wonderful source of love, support, and encouragement for their grandchildren. Though I do not share the physical traits of my parents, I would like to believe that I am a reflection of who they are and the values they have instilled in me. They will always share my heart.

Though I have and will continue to experience great struggles along my adoption journey, I feel at peace with my decision not to search. I will inevitably encounter days throughout my journey where I will miss what I never had. There will be days when I will grieve and mourn the loss of someone whose blood is running through my veins, but is a complete stranger to me. My birth mother missed out on my life and the person I have become. I often find it painful to think about her, knowing my feelings towards her will be ever changing. She brought me into this world, but I do not consider her the person who gave me life—my adoptive parents did that. She will never be the person I call "Mom," but she will forever be my birth mother and she will always have a place in my heart. I am okay with wondering about her and loving her from afar. I am okay with not knowing what I am missing and not searching in an effort to protect myself and my family from that potential pain of yet another rejection. Giving up that shred of hope has helped me to find a little peace and has allowed me to work on finding closure and healing my heart. I will never meet my birth mother, but I want her to know that I am okay and living the life I would like to think she wanted for me. I have an amazing family whom I love more than anything. My decision not to search has not been an easy one to make by any means, but for now, my heart is very full and my soul is at peace.

I Had the Perfect Adoptive Parents, and I Still Want to Search

Deanna Binkofsky

Deanna was was raised in Richmond Heights Ohio by Joe (1933) and Aggie Pullella (1936-2008). Her dad, a proud Italian from Little Italy, and mom, a Syrian Queen (at least that's what she told her family) loved shopping for antiques and cooking. Deanna's parents were always more than good to her. At about seven-years-old, her mom came to her with a children's book explaining adoption. They read it together and it was then that Deanna learned she was adopted. The author still has that book.

* * *

My Dad worked as an electrician, my Mom stayed home with me and my older brother, Joe (also adopted at birth, no not my "real" brother...I hate that question!). We had a fairy tale life, for the most part - spoiled rotten and loved and accepted by so many! I dropped out of high school my senior year, got my GED in 1996 and have been working at Progressive Insurance since 1999. My Husband and I married in 1998. We have four kids Alisandra, Gabrielle, Luke, and Joseph. We live Timberlake, Ohio, with our dogs Lola and Georgie.

I was about eight years old when my Adoptive Mom came to me in my perfectly pink room and told me I was special. She sat down on my bed with me and we read a book about adoption. It was a grey book with lots of pencil drawings and red swooshes to highlight shoes and dresses. I did not understand right away why she suddenly had the need, in the middle of the afternoon, to sit and read a book with me about adopted kids. But spending one-on-one time with her was just about my favorite thing to do, so I went along with it, for her sake of course. When we were done with the book, she looked at me and told me the truth; I was adopted. She was not my "real" mom, and my dad, well, he was not really my dad either. Tough stuff when you are eight.

Ok, maybe you should read that book again, Mom. I was really confused! How could I be adopted? I don't remember another family. I don't recall another life before this one. We were in my pink room with my bed and my stuff for heaven's sake. This IS my family. A tear streamed down her face, and she left me to absorb this absurd idea. I remember going to her room a while later and asking questions: Who is she? Where is she? When can I meet her? How did you get me? What did I do wrong? Why didn't she want me? I also asked about my older brother, was he also adopted? Her startling answer was yes, and for some reason that made me feel better. At least I wasn't alone.

I spent my young life playing with neighbors in the woods, catching frogs, swimming, playing softball, spending time with friends and thinking about Her. My adoptive mom and dad have never let me down. They have given me everything. My parents have sacrificed everything for my brother and me. We had a good life. We went to Catholic school, went to church every Sunday, and visited with my Dad's sister, my God-Mother, almost every week. My grandma lived with her, so my uncles and their families would visit there too. My Mom's family lived a little further away, but we spent time with them as often as possible and would always spend holidays with them. We held up family traditions and ate the tastiest Italian and Syrian food you could ever sink your teeth into. The adults would play cards after dinner, and my cousins and I would play until someone (usually me, I was the only girl!) got a black eye or whined about watching football. *How could this not be my family?*

As I grew up, I started to notice little differences. My light frizzy hair and blue eyes in contrast to their beautifully coiffed black hair and dark eyes. The sunburn I would no doubt be pained with every summer, while their olive skin was tanned and sun-kissed. Their ease with one another, I did not have any real relationship with them unless I was babysitting for their kids. I was a lot younger than most of my cousins; as a matter of fact, I was younger than some of their kids too.

I felt angry, betrayed and hurt, not by my Mom and Dad, but by the hand that life dealt me. I had no one to place this blame on, so I blamed myself, and I hated myself for it. In my mind, I was such a horrible baby that she didn't want me. The conversations that I needed, didn't happen because no one seemed to know that I was sad and angry because I needed to know who She is, a name, a picture, anything. I could not ask for these things without feeling like I was breaking my mom and dad's hearts. I needed to talk about Her, but it was never right; I would not hurt them. They didn't do anything wrong; they were so good to me. They looked past my poor behavior and just loved me.

I cannot remember a time when I felt like I was treated differently by my family. Now as an adult, I wonder why I did not get into trouble for some of the decisions I made. Now as an adult and a parent, I wonder if some things just slid by because my Mom and Dad did not want me to say THOSE WORDS. I cannot recall ever saying THOSE WORDS, but I can imagine the fear of hearing them. *"You're not my real Mom and Dad"*.

They are my real parents. They taught me to walk, to eat, to wipe when I go to the potty. They built the roof over my head. They supplied the overpriced clothes on my back. They put delicious food in my belly. They made good decisions for my life. So if all of that is true… why was this woman still on my mind every day of my life?

I was very young when I decided I needed to find Her, but what can you do when you are ten? I figured I would wait until I was older and just go get my original birth certificate, what could possibly go wrong? Needing to know where I came from peaked just after I turned 18. My birth certificate had the name of the hospital where I was born, it also had the doctor's name that was there for my birth. I made two phone calls. The first was to 411 (the number we used to call for information before the internet). I asked for the number to the hospital and then asked for the doctor's office number. Sitting in my room with my pretty pink princess phone, I knew I was about to get some answers. The excitement was overwhelming!

The second phone call I made burst my bubble pretty quickly. I called the hospital and asked for the records department. The woman who answered the phone kindly told me that it was impossible for her to give me any of the information I wanted because the state of Ohio sealed those records after my adoption was finalized. I asked if the doctor would have this information. She said no and even if he did, he would not be allowed to share the information with me. Devastated, I hung up the phone. It was 1990, I did not know of any other avenues to take. I thought Private Investigators were for rich people (Thanks, Magnum!) I did not know I could order my non-identifying information; I did not know the adoption agency may have some information. I didn't know, and I could not hurt the people that I love, that loved me. I could not break their hearts; I could not ask for their help.

I don't think it was a secret anymore though, they knew I was curious about my birth family. I was not unhappy in any way with the life I was living; nobody did anything wrong. It took me a long time to figure out why it was so important to me. A piece of my puzzle was missing. I love puzzles, word puzzles, number puzzles, jigsaw puzzles, I have always been fascinated by the missing link. My dad loved to give me puzzles and show me tricks to help me remember my math facts. It was always fun and ironically, it was one of the bonds that I had with my dad all through my life, we love solving puzzles and riddles. There was no going to bed until we figured them out

I needed my missing piece. That is my best answer. If my adoptive parents and family were so accepting and so "perfect", why did I need to search? There has been a longing in my soul ever since I can remember. A feeling that I could not talk about without becoming overly emotional. I cried many nights over the course of my life fantasizing about Her. Do I have any siblings? Did she give me a name? I wanted to know about my heritage, their traditions, and of course my medical history. Do I have a life expectancy past today?

When you get down to the last ten pieces of a jigsaw puzzle and you realize there are only nine displaced pieces... When you are looking for last that word in the newspaper word search and it is just that elusive... When your Sudoku game is not adding up right... That is how I felt for 43 years four months and five days. I could hardly wait another minute to make that phone call.

There is no way to make a biological child understand what being adopted feels like. An adopted friend of mine made this analogy: Imagine that you are eight years old and your mom tells you that the one thing you really want is stashed away and you can't have it. You tear up your house and your life, you search every corner of the small part of the world you know, and then you are forced by nature to just deal with never having it. You can only make the best with what you have. You come to terms with your loss and move on. In time, for some of us, it becomes an enigma.

I have always been proud of being adopted. My parents made me feels special and were upfront about anything I asked, but if I did not ask, I did not need to know. My mom did not really volunteer information and it was something I never really talked about with my dad. However, when I was older, he was the one that gave me the little bit of information I had. We were at the bank, he was adding my name to his safe deposit box. When he looked inside he said "oh this has your name on it, I think it's your adoption papers".(WHHHAAATTT!!!) "Oh ok, thanks!" Holding back the tears in the bank, in the car, and into the house, frantic to see what information it would bestow upon me, this was the pot of gold at the end of the rainbow!! I waited again. I was never a patient person; I felt as though it was actually killing me! When we got home I scrambled up to my room and opened the envelope as quickly as I could! It wasn't much, but it was more than I ever had and I was so appreciative for it. I tried to connect what little I had but still did not have a name, a city, or an idea of where to start.

My Dad, my Hero, the one person I could always count on for everything and anything, had just given me my next set of clues. He knew it was important to me, he knew how much it meant to me. He also knew *what* it meant. I was going to find Her. He seemed ok with that, he seemed grounded to that. What could I possibly do with this little bit of information? The internet was years away from my fingertips. I was sure there was somewhere I could go for help, but I had no idea who to call or where to go. Again, I just waited and hoped, always asking myself why this was so important. Wondering if she was looking for me.

Faces in a crowd, faces at church, faces in the mall. Voices on the phone, in movies, and music; which ones belonged to me? Not knowing was always too much for me. How is it ok that some huge percentage of the population knew everything there was to know about who and where they came from, and there I sat. It becomes a mantra: *I have a family. I love my family. My family is good. They love me, they accept me, I am theirs, and they are mine.* But really, do biological kids ever go through this? Do biological kids ever wonder if people only like them because they were born into their family? Do biological kids ever worry that if they are bad or if they screw up they will be sent back to where they came from....not knowing where the hell they came from?

There were plenty of things I took for granted. Plenty of moments that being adopted did not even cross my mind, but whenever it did, it was never because of something someone said. It was just a lost emotion. Friends with sisters (do I have any?) Wanting another sibling (the family next door had eight kids, can't I have one!) I needed to look like someone, smile like someone, laugh and feel like these things were a part of me. Like I was a part of them. Not the "adopted fool". I have been called many things and have cried many times over being called some mean thing or another, but that one I will never forget, that one is the unforgivable. It was my brother's friend's little brother, which made it even worse. It stopped being just me getting picked on and made to cry, it was him now too. I looked up to him, he was the person I wanted to mirror, now he was just like me; an adopted fool. I didn't tell anyone about that. I needed to forget it ever happened. Unfortunately, it is the one thing I will never be able to forget.

On April 3rd, 2015, I got a phone call at work from my husband, the envelope from the Ohio Bureau of Vital Statistics had arrived in the mail. My heart suddenly in my throat, tears streaming down my face, the hair on my arms on end, every bit of me buzzing and incoherent, I drove home from work. I do not remember the drive; I do know that I should have probably let someone drive for me! I tore into the house and saw it sitting in front of the computer. I touched it, took a picture of it, and posted the picture on Facebook with the caption "It's here!" I cried. I could not breathe. I looked at my husband and could not make the decision to open it. He was leaving for work, so he "gently encouraged me" to open it quickly so he would not be too late for his shift. If I said he was in complete disbelief that I froze at that moment, that would be an understatement. For weeks I had waited for this envelope. For days I had checked the mail two or three times a day, even after someone picked up the mail I would check again, just in case they missed something. Now I was sitting with it in my hand, 43 years, four months and four days in the making. Finally, I opened the envelope.

My given name was Kelly Anne. Her name and the address she lived at when I was born was listed. Her signature. Everything else was the same as my amended birth certificate, but I had a name and I knew her name. I decided that I did not *feel* like a Kelly Anne, but the satisfaction of having this in my hands was enough for the moment. My husband left for work. I made a few phone calls; I waited to call my dad until last. I was going to his house to make an Easter treat, so I just told him it came and I would bring it with me.

I did some research while we baked, but I did not find much. I was not sure where to start. Saturday morning though, I woke up feeling like the best Private Detective ever known to man! I had ideas and coffee; that is pretty much all it took too! I looked up her address from my original birth certificate on the county auditor's web site. I found my grandmother's name, she owned a restaurant - I like to cook! NICE! She had passed away two years before my mom. A normal person would have been upset; I on the other hand had an epiphany! Death Notices (please forgive my excitement!) On to Google! I found her obituary and there it was. Her name, names of my aunts and uncles, cousins, grandfather, sisters and brothers, nieces and nephews! The notice also said "of Arveda CO" after her name. I had hit the ever loving jackpot! One last quick Google search and I had two phone numbers!

I had to sum up some courage. I looked online at the "First Contact" information from Adoption Network Cleveland. I wrote out what I wanted to say; it was simple and to the point. The butterflies in my guts felt as though they were in a hurricane, my brain was mush. I picked up the phone and dialed the number – no longer in service, I dialed the other number – ringing, ringing, ringing – a man answered the phone. One huge gulp, I asked for her. He told me to hold on, she's outside. OH MY! OH MY! OH MY GAWD!!! I'D FOUND HER!!! She came to the phone and said "Hello". I asked her if she was busy, if now was a good time to talk, I had personal business to talk about with her. She lost her patience immediately with me (LOL… yep, I had the right person!) After a moment, I asked her if my birth date meant anything to her. You could hear a pin drop.

You could feel the tension ease. Every bit of me was shaking uncontrollably. She said "It means everything to me", and we cried, a lot! We still cry on the phone together some seven months later. She told me her husband's name. She told me I had two younger half-sisters and a half-brother along with two younger step-brothers and a step-sister. I am the oldest? Well that is new! We talked for about 25 minutes and we both needed a break. We hung up with the promise of another phone call tomorrow, Easter Sunday!

Easter came along with a much longer phone call! She told me she had sang Happy Birthday to me every year. She told me about her children, and she told me they did not know about me. I was her secret, and she asked that I did not post her name on Facebook just yet. I had my family over for the holiday dinner and told them everything I knew. Always supportive, always my hero, my dad was beside himself when I told him that my heritage was the same as his! I am Sicilian! We were sure that is why my sauce is so good! I sent her pictures of everyone and promised another call.

Our phone call on Monday took me by surprise. She said she was planning a trip to Cleveland on April 20th! BOOM!! I didn't see that coming! After a long stutter, I realized nothing could have made me happier! Her plan was to visit with her kids the day before her trip to tell them about me. She lives a few hours away from them and was not able to make the trip until then. I had to trust her, and we all know what happened the last time I trusted her!

Every possible scenario ran through my mind over the next two weeks. I had come to the conclusion that she was just baiting me. Telling me what I wanted, *needed*, to hear with no intention of ever telling my siblings about me. We talked and got to know each other almost every day, but the thought of her telling her grown children that they had another sister in Ohio that she never told them about loomed menacingly over me like the Grim Reaper. I did not feel worthy of her revealing this secret to the ones who most loved and trusted her. How could I expect her to break that trust after all this time?

Then on the evening of April 19th she called from her hotel. She said she talked to them, and they were excited to hear from me, would I mind if they called me? WOULD I MIND? Um, not at all! I had been stalking their Facebook pages, so I immediately went to send them friend requests only to find that both of my sisters had already found me… they found me! We chatted for a bit through text, and then finally I made the first phone call. It was exhilarating! To hear another voice like mine. My sister laughed *just like me*. I recognized it right away. My sister! We had a quick, wonderstruck conversation, one of the most amazing exchanges of words I have ever had! After I talked to her my heart was swelled, my eyes were wet, and my soul was free. A little while later (it is actually all a blur) I talked to my other sister and my brother; we had decided to Facetime so we could all see each other! Oh my goodness, I knew what they looked like from their pictures, but now I was going to put the faces to their voices, to put the laughs to the smiles. It was nothing less than the most beautiful moments of my life!

On April 20th, her plane was landing; we were meeting her at the airport. Her sister would be joining us there too. I have never felt so anxious! I can assume it is nothing less than waiting in the waiting room while your wife is having a baby! Every time an announcement came over the PA system I just knew it was her plane. Pacing, sitting, standing, wandering around and feeling an enormous change about to happen to my life. I trusted her and she did not let me down. Everything was coming together better than I could have ever hoped for.

She came down the escalator and we knew each other immediately. As my husband recorded the moment on my phone, we hugged for the first time. We touched each other's faces, kissed and hugged some more! We spent a wonderful week together. There were a couple hiccups with a rental car and me forgetting to bring my family with me for a visit at her sister's house, but there was never any question on her end. She accepted me and my family from the moment we first talked. After meeting her sister, I could feel how much I was missed. They had talked about me and prayed for me together every day. Prayed for me to call, prayed for me to be happy and healthy, and prayed that I would want them in our lives. I met my uncle, their children and two of their three grandchildren. Freckles!! Their son has freckles! I have some too, but nothing like my daughter. She has a field of freckles down her leg. We had always wondered who they came from, now, meeting my cousin I had no doubt. It was at that moment I realized they were supposed to have come with me. My kids should have been there meeting and playing with their cousins! My Aunt told me not to apologize, she said she understood how badly we both needed time together.

We went for a ride to see the house she grew up in, the neighborhood, the city. She talked a lot. Told me stories of her younger years and about her parents, but I had questions. I needed to hear the story of my birth.

My birth father never knew about me. He did not tell her he was a married man with three children at home until "after." She had no other information on him for me. (That's ok though, I am ok with that. One day maybe I will try DNA testing, but I have a new huge family to get to know, one thing at a time.) She also talked about how she had almost changed my grandfather's mind about keeping me, but my grandmother was stone. I was not meant to be a part of their family.

On the day I was born, her sister and mother were with her, they prayed and cried. She pleaded one last time. She said she saw my little red hair over the nurse's arm as she took me out of the room. By her choice, she never saw my face, she never touched me or held me. She could not say goodbye. I cannot imagine the pain.

In July, my husband and I gathered up three of our four kids and drove across the country to meet my siblings. It was a crazy trip! When we finally found our hotel and unpacked the car, there was nothing that could keep me away from them. They live right around the corner from where we were staying, a stone's throw after all this time. We pulled up in front of their home, and I could see my birth mom waving us in! They all ran down off the porch. One of my sisters was at work, but my other sister and brother were waiting for me with their arms open wide. Hugs and tears abounded! I met my nephew and my sister's husband. I met my birth mom's husband, the guy that could do no wrong, because HE answered the phone! We went in the house where I was introduced to my sibling's father. We ate and laughed. The kids all played together. Everything fell into place very easily. To me, it felt like we had known each other our whole lives. The conversation was never weird. The laughter did not feel forced. It was good! So, so good!

We went back to our hotel for some rest. A call on my phone woke me around midnight. My baby sister was outside waiting to meet me! I opened the door and said "hi"! Everyone else was asleep so I did not invite her in; we sat on the step and talked for a few minutes before determining that it was much warmer at her house. I hopped in her truck, we made a couple phone calls, and before I knew it, I was sitting in my sister's living room with both of my sisters and my brother! It was just the four of us, same blood, all four of us together for the first time! It was my favorite night of our trip. Just sitting there watching TV and chatting about whatever crossed our minds at the moment. Heavenly!

Something had been nagging at me throughout the week. I wanted an answer, but I felt like I was questioning someone's integrity, and rarely do I feel something is important enough to do that. This was one of those rare times. I asked my sibling's father if he thought things would have been different if he had met my birth mom and she had a baby in tow. He said no; he said he had fallen head over heels for her and nothing would have changed had she kept me. I was relieved that I would not have changed their lives, but I was sad at the same time. Could she have kept me? Could I have lived without the pain of being adopted, without being different or special?

I know now that I did not have a choice in the matter, and I know now that decisions were made "in my best interest". Since meeting my birth family this past summer, I have found that I am happy where I am, I am happy that I had the opportunities that were given to me and the opportunities that I am able to give to my own children. I don't know what my life would have been like growing up with six younger half/step brothers and sisters with my birth mom. I know I would not be who I am today and I would not have the people in my life that I cherish. Yet I miss my half-sisters and brother when we are apart. I love learning about them and spending time with them, even if it is a phone call or text message. I am also excited to share photos and stories with my birth mom. I like to learn about her life. I will have them now and forever. I love them all for who they are and for what they represent. They are my family now too. My pain has subsided and my heart is open!

Most of my family has been beyond supportive. My brother has not asked too many questions, and we have not talked much about it. He is not interested in finding his birth family. I would never push him; if he changes his mind, I will support him and help him along his journey any way I can. My oldest daughter has been very resistant to meeting my birth family. She really wants nothing to do with the whole thing. As much as it hurts me, I try not to force the issue. She has not really given me any reason; I have tried to explain to her why it is so important to me, but I have come to accept that she has no interest. It is all I can do.

My relationship with my dad has changed. It is a good change. I can definitively say that no one could ever make me feel more loved, more supported, or more confident. He has listened to my stories. He has looked at my pictures. When my decision to search was questioned by a family member, he stood by my side and comforted my tears. He chose not to meet her when she was here visiting in April, I could do nothing but completely understand; I am his and my mom's daughter, no matter what the blood says. He has taught me more about himself in the last seven months than in the last 40+ years. He has taught me to give of myself with no expectation, to love fully and unconditionally, and to trust, even when it hurts.

Thank you, Dad. To you, my hero, I dedicate this chapter.

Ethnicity Unknown

Lynn Grubb

Lynn Grubb is an adoptee and a parent by marriage, biology, and adoption. She writes for Lost Daughters, is the editor of *The Adoptee Survival Guide: Adoptees Share Their Wisdom and Tools*, and she contributes to various adoption anthologies. Lynn co-facilitates an adoption support group in her hometown of Dayton, Ohio and is also an adoptee rights advocate, hoping to educate the masses that adoptees deserve equal rights to their original birth certificates. You can visit her at her blog: www.noapologiesforbeingme.blogspot.com or contact her on Twitter @IllinoisAdoptee.

* * *

A quick Google search when I type the words, "ethnicity unknown," provided an Adoption.com forum post by Mystik on posing this question in the foster parent online support group:

Unknown Ethnicity Question

We're currently in the early Home Study process for adopting *B* & not that it really matters, but due to her unique situation we have no idea what her ethnicity is. The hospital marked her as "Hispanic" based on general looks as a newborn, but as she's gotten older she's obviously changed quite a bit and I'm not so sure. As annoying as it is I also get asked all the time what her ethnicity is and then I start feeling like a bumbling idiot either trying to explain we don't know without going into detail or to make things simple I just say "Hispanic". I've had many people I know say she looks like she could be part "AA" or maybe "(Puerto Rican)". But who knows? Again it's not something I really feel is of any major importance to us, we love her like crazy regardless, but what if she wants to know herself when she gets older?

Reading this I instantly thought, *"Now there is a parent who gets it."*

The focus is not so much on the parent's need to know, but the realization that the *child* will grow up one day and want to know. Very astute and very true. Several years ago, I posted an essay at Lost Daughters titled "On Being Generic Ethnic" in which I discuss how I identified with being Italian for a large portion of my adult life despite having very little evidence that this was true. The essay described my journey and feelings about other people telling me who I am (i.e. you are probably Italian, Greek, Spanish, Lebanese, etc.) compared to who I believed I was and my struggle, similar to Mystik's in the post above, on whether to tell the truth *(i.e. "I just don't know")* or to make up an ethnicity for the simplicity of conversation.

Glossing over the issue always felt inauthentic to me, so I usually just said I was adopted and did not know, which prompted more questions. The phrase "genealogical bewilderment"[1] comes to mind as I really and truly did not know anything about where I came from. Growing up having this truth withheld from me struck me as deeply unjust.

Having no information about my background for the first 25 years of my life felt disorienting. I was always very open with others about my being adopted, which then prompted the cycle of questions about where I came from. Apparently, it was evident to others that I had this "ethnic" look about me prompting one friend to refer to me as "generic ethnic". When I told people the truth, I felt "less than" and ashamed of not knowing the answers. Because I felt I could not completely identify with my adoptive family's ethnic background, even though we did share a mixed European ethnicity, I felt unrooted, unreal, false, and not like others. I tried to push the feelings away; however, they always returned each time somebody asked me about my background. It felt very unfair to me that other kids and adults knew the answers about their background, but not only did I not know, I had

---

[1] **Genealogical bewilderment** is a term referring to potential identity problems that could be experienced by a child who was either fostered, adopted or conceived via an assisted reproductive technology procedure such as surrogacy or gamete donation (egg or sperm donation).https://en.wikipedia.org/wiki/Genealogical_bewilderment

no way of knowing due to the laws. Until I got a bit older and more mature, I felt disempowered with this aspect of my life.

My parents had no idea of my ethnicity or anything else about my background, nor did they ask any questions to those in authority when I was growing up. My parents were just so happy to have me—and later my brother— they would have never questioned the agency for fear of being deemed ungrateful for providing them with a family.

So I walked around with an unknowable, unnamable, phantom type of pain. I was good at hiding this pain, and it went undetected by my mother. I could never put the pain into words, and I gave my mother the impression that I was unemotional in general and "didn't care" about much (in truth, I am very sensitive and would likely be labeled a Highly Sensitive Person). I mostly felt invalidated by my mother growing up, as if she was unable to get outside of her own viewpoints to really "see me" or "understand me". Invalidation is a life theme for me and one that has been the core of many of my blogs. As an adoptee, I have felt a lifelong invalidation from not only my parents, but laws, the media, adoption agencies, adoption attorneys, and the general public. With that much invalidation flowing into your life, it is a wonder anybody musters up the courage to search.

One vivid memory stands out for me. I was 22 or so and my mother and I went to the World A'Fair held at the Dayton Convention Center every year. I remember looking around at all the different countries represented there: China, Germany, Mexico, Ireland, Greece, etc., feeling this deep yearning as I watched the people do their cultural dances, serve their delicious foods, and sell their home-made crafts.

I wondered to myself, *"How was it possible that all of these people knew their roots, and not only knew, but celebrated them openly?"* How fortunate they were without even knowing it! I wanted to run up to each of them and ask, *"How does it feel to be part of a culture, an ethnicity, and know that you are deeply rooted in tradition and blood?"* I longed for what I perceived was their sense of belonging and cultural identity.

The pain I experienced that monumental day brought home to me that even as an adult, I still had absolutely no idea where I fit into the grand scheme of things. This was a turning point for me in questioning the status quo. I would no longer accept non-answers and being powerless. I did not know it then, but I was on the verge of seeking the truth. Within just a couple years of that fateful day, I contacted my adoption agency for the first time.

Reflecting back on that day, I asked myself, "What was the most painful aspect of it?" I recall that even though I felt brave enough to share my desires with my mom (that I wanted to find my birth mother), I did not receive the validation that I had hoped for. My mom looked at me and then proceeded to tell me a horror story she had heard about an adoptee who tracked down her birth mother. This particular birth mother never told her husband about relinquishing a child, so you can imagine (or so the story went) that this sudden appearance of the adoptee, ruined this birth mother's life. I was dumbfounded that my mother told me this story. And in my usual defensive attitude, I retorted, *"Well, it's her own fault for lying."*

Not being a parent myself at that time and still somewhat in the adoption "fog" (see: Lost Daughters roundtable: "Emerging from the Fog"), I had no direct awareness that my mother felt deeply threatened by my discussing a potential search for my birth mother. The question that strikes me now is this: *Why could my mother not identify with my pain of not knowing?* And the answer I have come up with as a mother myself now is this: *She was more concerned about her own perceived losses than the losses I was experiencing.*

I recently asked my mom why she never asked the agency any questions. I was born during the Baby Scoop Era, a period in American and Western European history starting after the end of World War II and ending in the early 1970s characterized by an increased rate of pre-marital pregnancies over the preceding period, along with a higher rate of newborn adoption. Back in the BSE, questions were discouraged and apparently truth was not as important as making a child sound good to adoptive parents. My mother has stated to me that in the seventies, there were a lot of stories in the media about birth parents who re-claimed children they relinquished, which fueled the fears of adoptive parents everywhere. I imagine she had conflicted feelings about raising someone else's child—I know I was full of those conflicted feelings when my husband and I adopted.

I understand the laws (then and now) prohibit agencies from disclosing certain things, but I still cannot come to any sort of resolution in my mind and heart as to how you can place a child in a new family without ever providing adoptive parents with more than a scrap of information. The scrap I had was this: *"your mother was artistic."* I did not even know in what way she was artistic. All questions I asked my parents were met with, *"We just don't know."*

I am sure having an unusually curious child that you had no answers for frustrated my parents to no end. However, it never prompted them to seek out the information, to question the agency, attorney, or the State of Illinois, or to become creative like a friend of mine (an adoptive parent) who paid a private investigator in Russia to find out her adopted daughter's beginnings and to even get a photo of her daughter's birth mother. She stated to me the impetus for this endeavor, *"I imagined my daughter would one day want to look into the face of the woman who gave birth to her at least once."*

My mother was probably terrified on some level that if she did one wrong thing, if she asked one wrong question to the agency, they may take my brother or I back, or it could provoke mine or my brother's birth mother to show up on her doorstep. I can only guess because, although I have had many conversations with my mother, she is a tough cookie to get answers from. She still has this undying loyalty to the agency from where I was adopted – half a century later. I think about how our relationship could have been so much better, had she just validated my need for truth and supported me in seeking it.

I understand my parents did not receive the proper education, and they do get a pass for adopting during the closed era at a time where children were thought (hoped) to be blank slates. But we are now in the era of open adoption (just the term "open" causes people to believe that records are also open; most are still sealed and protected by law) where we are (hopefully) educated enough to understand that every child comes with their own unique set of genetics and will be individually unique in his reaction to those genetics and the environment in which he is raised.

I have heard Oprah say, "When you know better, you do better" (Attributed to Maya Angelou). One way to do better is to provide adopted children and adults with factual information about their backgrounds, including their ethnicity. For adoption to be truly ethical, it needs to be accepted wisdom that adopted children or others separated from original family not only have a need but a right to know where they come from and why they were relinquished or removed from their families of origin.

I wish my parents had been provided with information such that David Brodzinsky discusses in *The Psychology of Adoption:*

"The search therefore constitutes the adoptee's attempt to repair a sense of loss, relieve the sense of disadvantage, consolidate identity issues including body image and sexual identity, resolve cognitive dissonances, internalize the locus of control, and satisfy the most fundamental need to experience human connectedness."

After spending most of my life in an ethnic-limbo, if you will, I am pleased to report that I am now feeling grounded and rooted to the human race. Thanks to genetic genealogy, in 2013, I sent my DNA to three companies: Family Tree DNA, 23 and Me, and Ancestry. Each of these autosomal DNA tests provided me with an ethnic ancestry breakdown. Imagine my surprise when I learned I was barely Italian (less than two-percent) but very Spanish and 29% Native American (you can read about my genetic genealogy journey at both my blog or in The Adoptee Survival Guide).

It has been three years since that discovery, and I feel I am still digesting this new reality slowly but eagerly. In hindsight, it all makes sense. The time when the creepy attorney I once worked for called me a "hot Latin woman" in the middle of a staff meeting or why people kept confusing me with one of my former supervisors who is half German/half Mexican. Suddenly old friends were admitting to me they always thought I looked Latina. Being suddenly Latina, was a shock, but a welcome surprise.

My daughter and I went back to the World A'Fair this year and this experience was completely different. Instead of pain, I was excited to be there sharing this amazing event with my daughter. I visited the countries of my background: Germany, Mexico, Ireland, and Colombia. We visited the countries of my daughter's ethnic background and explored and shared many different cultures, foods, and dances that day.

That happy memory has replaced the sad memory of invalidation and all the years of not knowing. At fifty-years-of-age, I now feel rooted and grounded, and I know without a shadow of a doubt that I share a sense of belonging with my fellow human beings.

116

REFERENCES

Baby Scoop Era, http://babyscoopera.com/home/what-was-the-baby-scoop-era.

Grubb Lynn. "The Reluctant Latina."
http://noapologiesforbeingme.blogspot.com/2014/08/the-reluctant-latina-how-dna-test-can.html

The Psychology of Adoption, pp. 88-89, 1990, edited by David M. Brodzinsky, Associate Professor of Development and Clinical Psychology Rutgers University, Marshall D. Schecter, Professor of Child and Adolescent Psychiatry of Pennsylvania School Medicine (Emeritus).

Adoptee Health Issues

Karen Belanger

Karen Belanger is an adult adoptee and the author of "Assembling Self" an adoption poetry book and writes at her blog of the same name. She has contributed at The Lost Daughters bloggers and is included in the *Lost Daughters Anthology* as well as *Adoption Therapy* books. She has a piece published in the book, *The Adoptee Survival Guide* and is now working on her second book. She inherited her biological mother's love of dance, cooking from scratch, growing roses, and her great grandmother's musical talent. Karen is the mother of three grown children and in her spare time she also enjoys reading, working out, and helping other adoptees on their paths towards healing."

* * *

I was adopted when I was two-weeks-old. I was told about adoption when I was around five and never really could comprehend what "adopted" meant other than I was not with the mother who gave birth to me. I had no idea where my biological family was or why they had given me away. My younger adopted brother had no real words to speak of about being adopted. I asked questions but there were no real answers. I was shamed into not asking at a very young age.

I was a bouncy, bubbly, active child. In fact I was doing gymnastics since before I can remember and earned the title "Cartwheel" at the age of about seven. I think until the age of puberty my favorite way to get anywhere was not on my feet; I was either somersaulting or flipping or walking on my hands. I loved swimming, golf, softball, tennis, and a good game of neighborhood kickball. Nothing could stop me from the athletic nature I had and boundless energy. Little was I aware that life can change and change quickly.

The demise of my health began at the age of fifteen, during my sophomore year in high school. I had not begun my monthly cycle as all of my other friends had, and I was not developing either. I spoke to my mother who finally took me to the doctor who promptly put me on medication to start the process. The meds made me extremely ill for days with vomiting, weakness, and pain; however, it did what it was supposed to do, and soon I officially became a woman.

But all did not go well for me from there. I began to bleed without stopping, and by the time my medical issues were acknowledged I was very ill. I was anemic to the point of being nonfunctional. My experience was not normal at all; however, not really knowing what normal should be, I had no comparative value to what other girls were really experiencing. Being very involved in school and extracurricular activities including competitive gymnastics I pushed through because I hated missing out on what I loved, and I loved school, athletics, and music.

I began to experience an inability to focus on school work, exhaustion, abdominal pain, and fainting spells. I ended up in the school nurse's office often, and my grades slipped as I began to be unable to complete assignments or even function as I used to. I tried to tell my parents, but I had been accused of faking it and trying to skip school. I was scared and afraid and with the lack of understanding from my parents, I kept all of it to myself. I was flunking out of school. Fortunately, since I had been an excellent student prior to this, my teachers all confronted me, and my parents were notified of my ill health.

By the time I got to the doctor I was very extremely anemic. I was put on heavy doses of iron, rest, and birth control pills. I would be diagnosed at the age of 29 with polycystic ovarian disease and find out later my biological mother had surgery for ovarian cysts at the same age I was when I began to suffer from the disease.

My health improved, and I was busy enjoying every minute of it. By the time I was a senior I was working part-time in a busy three star restaurant, involved in band, orchestra, several musical groups, dance team, and church group, plus I had an active social life. I graduated from high school and had a bright outlook on the future and college.

Then, that summer I contracted mononucleosis. I had been working long hours at the restaurant and began to feel ill, extremely ill. When I did not get better I went to the doctor who told me I was so sick that if I did not get better they were going to do emergency surgery to remove my spleen because it was so infected. My liver was not fairing much better. Being afraid of the hospital, I went to the doctor every day to have blood taken to make sure I would not have to be hospitalized. I remained in bed unable to function for the majority of a month.

Other friends came down with mononucleosis however, they got sick and were better in a matter of days with the exception of one who was as ill as I was. I did not drink, smoke, or do any kinds of drugs; there was zero reason for me to become that sick. I can honestly tell you that since that illness I have never regained the energy and health I had prior to becoming ill. I have lived the rest of my life with the need to sleep more, rest more, and not be able to adhere to work, social, and activities others are able to fairly easily accomplish. I was later diagnosed with chronic fatigue syndrome finally at the age of 36.

Fast forward to age 23; I was in college, and I became pregnant with my first child. All the thoughts of my birth mother came to the forefront. Here I was single, pregnant, and on my own. By the time I found out I was pregnant there were no other options. I married the father because that was what was expected. It was at that point I wanted to know my birth mother for real, talk to her, ask her questions, and find out if she felt as I did when she found out she was pregnant out of wedlock. I turned to ALMA Adoptees' Liberty Movement Association, the only adoptee search organization I had ever heard of; I signed up but never received any response.

I ended up with toxemia of pregnancy and the swelling during labor cost me a broken tail bone in child birth. I collapsed a few days after giving birth, unable to walk. I have lived my life since in extreme back pain that has progressively worsened with time and age. I now have degenerative disc and spine disease which was compounded by gymnastics injuries and working with small children on my feet for years.

Soon after the birth of my first child, I began to notice nausea after eating meals. It was fairly mild, and I ignored it, choosing to eat a little less than others did. After the birth of my second child five years later it became extremely difficult to eat anything of substance, and I began occasionally vomiting when I ate too much, what would be considered a regular meal for most people. Slowly over time it worsened to the point that I was living on crackers, soup, and milk and only in small portions. I ended up weighing 99 pounds, and I am 5' 6" tall. I was hospitalized and diagnosed with anorexia and bulimia. I tried to convince the doctors that I loved food, but it fell on deaf ears. I signed myself out of the hospital knowing I was not anorexic or bulimic.

I did have one doctor who finally asked me about my lack of family medical history. I told him I was adopted and was asked to get updated family medical history as they could not help me further because my symptoms of extreme fatigue, vomiting, and malaise had no identifiable cause(s). But, my question was "records from where?" It was pre-internet, and the only thing I could figure out was that I would probably have to petition a judge where my adoption was finalized. But again, finalized where?

I asked my adoptive parents and told them doctors were requesting family medical background, but I got nowhere with it. My adoptive mother claimed to not remember where I was adopted or what hospital I was born in, and my adoptive father refused to discuss the issue at all. With no other adoptee resource around, I was stymied in my attempts to get any decent family medical history, let alone anything current. I simply gave up.

My health issues prevailed, and I got to the point where I could not function, at least not for any length of time or enough to hold a regular job. I was told I was a hypochondriac, crazy, attention seeker, or that I was a drug addict due to the weight loss from the lack of being able to eat much. My life revolved around trying to act and look normal, while isolating myself from everyone who labeled or judged my life, or lack thereof. I was living on crackers, milk, soup, and not much else or even much of those because too much would mean losing all of it in the sink.

My weight was so low my friends jokingly nicknamed me "Skeletor." It was funny to them, but it wasn't funny to me. And, I had no answers to the questions I kept asking myself "Why do I feel this bad?", "Why am I so ill all the time?", and "where is my biological family and the answer to my health mysteries?" No answers came.

While pregnant with my last child, I began to go into early labor at five and a half months. The next few months were spent in and out of the hospital with doctors doing everything to stop the early labor. I was on medication and bed rest most of the pregnancy. I could barely eat anything at all and spent my days knowing I had to keep enough food down for my baby's sake. My son thankfully was born full weight and healthy; however, I was not healthy - far from it. The next year my ability to eat tanked. I arose each morning to throw up in the sink, get a cup of coffee, and spend my day caring for my son, home, and husband as best as I could. I weighed 107 pounds by this time.

My saving grace at that point in time was decent health insurance through my husband's job. I began going to the doctor who finally referred me to a gastroenterologist and an internal specialist. The next two months were spent in and out of testing, sonograms, blood work, MRIs, CAT scans, more blood workup, and more tests until finally I was sent to a surgeon who said "Oh I talk to people like you all day; it's your gall bladder. We are taking it out." He was snide and dismissive and I was LIVID. I told him about the years I had spent ill, the loss of jobs, relationships, time and energy in and out of health facilities and with physicians who told me it was all in my head or that I was mentally ill. Most of my health issue nightmare would have been preventable with accurate family medical history!

My surgery was scheduled two weeks later, and two days after I was up eating eggs, bacon, and anything I wanted. Three weeks later I was back to work. My gall bladder disease came with no stones. It was rare and only 6% of people with gall bladder disease suffer from it. There was nothing to show on a test, not until the very last test they did to dictate gall bladder disease exclusively. I now also know that this type of disease is commonly hereditary.

Although I was much healthier, I was still not really well, and my son was an extreme asthmatic. My time was not spent on trying to fix my remaining health issues but keeping my son as healthy as he could be. I still had the PCOS, CFS, and back issues to deal with while I tried to work and raise a family. I not only looked healthy, I looked good especially for my age. My looking good was very deceptive. I did not feel good, ever, and that was an understatement. I knew I needed current family medical information but from where and how?

I had gone back to college and was working full-time, going to school part-time, doing the normal wife and mother things like grocery shopping, cooking, cleaning, laundry, spending time with the kids and family, while care-taking for an ill child; it all began to take its toll. My marriage began to fall apart, and we wound up in marriage counseling. I was fortunate enough to get an adoptive mother as a marriage counselor, well versed in the issues of adoption not just professionally but personally with her adopted daughter. She was the first person who told me I needed to search and to find the answers I was seeking and not just medically, but because I had a RIGHT to that information. It was liberating to say the least to be encouraged to do what I had always wanted to do - find my biologically family! But, again, search where?

Enter the internet. My husband told me he had heard of people finding one another on the internet. One day in 1998, I typed "Adoptee" into the yahoo search engine, and VOILA a whole new world opened up for me. I found a Missouri state-specific search group to assist me with my search. My adoptive parents were still not forthcoming with any information about my adoption. I utilized the attending physician on my amended birth certificate, and within a week of joining the group, I found the doctor who witnessed my birth.

When I looked at the monitor with that information on the screen I broke down and wept, sobbing to a point I thought I would pass out. My three year old son came into the room and I only stopped when I saw the fear in his eyes that something was very very wrong with his mother. It was not that there was something wrong, there was something very right. I had finally found someone who not only knew who my mother was, but knew who I was before I was born. My search finally had a starting point.

I petitioned the county where I believed my adoption had been processed, and they found my adoption file. It was much to my surprise and amazement that I had to get my adoptive parents permission before the courts would do a search for my biological family for updated medical information even though I was 39 years old! My adoptive parents were not supportive at all. They said they needed time to think about the ramifications of my searching, what I would find, and if they could "allow" me." I was still in shock that I was an adult and had to request parental permission to attempt to receive my own family medical history even with a letter from my primary physician requesting updated medical information.

Upon my court petition my biological mother was found. I wrote a letter through the court as suggested by the court confidential intermediary handling my file. Due to the fact that I was a secret child and no one knew about me, my biological mother responded with updated medical records first. Later she sent a non-identifying letter and 40th birthday card; however, she would not sign the release of her name and address, requesting time to tell everyone about my existence including her children.

I found out that PCOS, endometriosis, heart attack, thyroid issues, and anxiety disorders ran on her side of the family. My biological grandparents had died at a young age from uterine cancer and heart attack, and my mother had surgery at age 15 for PCOS. Wouldn't that have been nice to tell doctors decades ago to save me the agony of being undiagnosed, misdiagnosed, un-medicated, or over-medicated?

My biological mother went back into hiding and requested no further communication be sent. I was devastated. The reunion she alluded to in her letters would never be. The courts could not locate my biological father. They would find him a few years later, but he denied any family medical information nor did he want contact.

After blood work, my doctor said my thyroid levels were not normal, and I needed to see an endocrinologist for further testing. My husband lost his job and our insurance before I could pursue the testing that I needed. A divorce shortly after that deemed there would be no answers to my thyroid issues as there was no insurance left to depend on.

There was little money to survive on, let alone spend on health insurance, co-pays, or medications. Most of what I have is pre-existing and even with insurance not affordably treatable. I lived in a state where access to affordable healthcare did not exist, and I was denied Medicaid. I was also taking care of an extremely ill asthmatic child with expensive medications.

I had premature labor and toxemia with all three of my pregnancies. I was hospitalized because my insides were a mess with PCOS and Endometriosis. My gall bladder was infected, dying, and shooting poison all through my system but they could not "see" it on screens from MRI's and CT scans. I have CFS and my thyroid has been whacking in and out since age 35 wracking havoc on my energy levels. I was diagnosed with scoliosis young then broke my back in child birth and slowly my spine and discs are degenerating from my neck through my sacral region and hips. I have bone and joint issues which might be Rheumatoid Arthritis, high blood pressure, and sometimes I do not even know how I have survived this long.

A great majority of what I have experienced was highly preventable and treatable with family medical history knowledge. Adoptees in most states are kept from obtaining most if not any information about their biological background and genetics. Knowledge is power as they say, but adoptees are expected to navigate life and survive without it. Our children suffer without accurate family medical and genetic history, as do their children. The chain of pain is continual and does not end with us.

Adoptees are continually told to be grateful for having a family and ridiculed for desiring only what everyone else has or at least a right to pursue the knowledge of. We are labeled as angry, emotionally unbalanced, or the very worst ungrateful we were not aborted. I cannot tell you how many thousands of times in my life I did wish my mother had that option. I do not believe this was the life she had planned for me, but it was the life the system of adoption handed me.

I am about to embark on my fifth or sixth court petition; I have lost track over the last seventeen years. I know what the outcome will probably be, but I will never give up hope, or hope for my children, that I will same day have the right to access MY family history and information. Rights and relationships are, and always will be, two separate issues. But, adoptees should have equal rights as all other citizens do. Until then, I will continue to funnel my energy into writing and educating about adoptee rights.

I am now fifty-six-years-old and only have half of what I know to be my current family medical history. I battle multiple hereditary and genetic disease and illnesses on a daily basis, undiagnosed until years after they had taken a toll. I still do not know if there are psychological or addiction issues which run in our family which have seemed to have affected me and my children. I do not know what runs on my father's side of the family; he denies me any information. Considering the state adoption laws in Missouri, I might never have that information to pass down to my children or their children and so on. I am angry. I should be. Who wouldn't be? Anger can eat you alive or it can be a powerful motivator to facilitate change in the world. It is your choice how to use it. I choose change.

The Impact of Silently Discouraging Searching

Lucy Sheen

Made in Hong Kong and exported to the UK as a transracial adoptee. Lucy is a dyslexic actor, published writer, filmmaker, trainer and transracial adoptee advocate. She loves Dim sum and Yorkshire puddings. Her first professional job was the female lead in the British feature film *PING PONG* (1987), the first ever UK feature to look at the history and issues of the British-Chinese community. Other films credits include: *Secrets & Lies* (1996), *Something Good: The Mercury Factor* (2013). Theatre credits include: Julius Caesar-Bristol Old Vic (1987); Drink the Mercury nominated for a TMA (first British East Asian actress to be so nominated in1990); Hungry Ghosts Tim Luscombe, nominated an OFFIE (Of West End) for best actress 2010. Plenty directed by the award Thea Sharrock (2011). TV credits include: Prime Suspect 2; Eastenders; Lovejoy and Nighty Night series 2. Radio credits include: Words On A Night Breeze, Bound Feet and Western Dress. Lucy's documentary Abandoned, Adopted, Here is available on YouTube. She's finished a writing commission for the renowned Royal Court Theatre in central London,

Restrain your grief and adapt to the mishap and is
working on two new full-length plays. Her next
performance is an excerpt from *Ungrateful-A Paper
Daughter on The Southbank.*

* * *

If you are a transracial adoptee, anything remotely like
me, then it is entirely probable that you were well
into your middle years, before actively and
consciously harboring thoughts about searching for your
birth family. For me, the idea, even the notion of
searching for my birth family was an alien concept. It had
been drummed into me by my adoptive parents,
especially my adoptive mother that inquiring about my
past and my birth family was not only futile, it was in
some way a negative act. My adoptive parents made it
known in no uncertain terms that asking questions about
my adoption would not be tolerated. What little
"information" they did share was scant and
uninformative.

I was told my by adoptive mother that there was no
information about me. My biological mother had
abandoned me. I was an unwanted baby. The implication
being I had more than likely been born out of wedlock. I
had be told throughout my childhood there was nothing
to know. As a young child I had been actively
discouraged and reprimanded for asking about my
circumstances and how I came to be adopted. After a
while I stopped openly asking questions. It was not until I
was approached, out of the blue in 2008, by BAAF

(British Association for Adoption and Fostering) with an invitation to participate in a research study about a group of Hong Kong foundlings who were adopted in the late 50s and early 60s. Apparently I was part of this group which was news to me!

I knew that I had been adopted. Even if, ludicrous as this might sound, my Caucasian adoptive parents were unwilling to acknowledge this fact. I also knew I had come over with other orphans from Hong Kong, but this was the first time I had ever heard anything about being part of an organized program of transracial adoptions. It was, as they say a, "no brainer." I agreed to participate in the research and in doing so opened a door.

First of all I would like to dispel some of the misnomers, sublimely held assumptions, caricatures, stereotypes, and tropes that have become accepted truths in the wider society, concerning transracial adoptees. As a transracial adoptee, I am like any other human being who is part of a specific group in society. I experience the full range of emotions, just the same as a child raised by his or her birth parents. I am subject to the same stimuli, the same dangers, the same positives and negatives. The difference being, I grew up in a familial unit that I am not genetically, culturally, or racially related to. Society tends to lump all transracial adoptees together, and they expect us, the adoptees, to be eternally grateful for having been adopted. Just because one may only have been exposed to positive stories of transracial adoption, does not mean that negative experiences do not exist or are not experienced by the adoptee. We must value and acknowledge the adult adoptees voice even if the story that is being told does not confirm to what we have been used to, expect, or perceive. It does not give one the right to dismiss or discount an adult adoptee's life story.

There is also the misunderstanding that the act of transracially adopting a child is in some way an act of salvation, that the child being adopted, is being rescued and elevated from a race and culture that is inferior and subservient to the (usually) white, middle-class, well educated, and financially comfortable adoptive family. There is an ingrained presumption in the West by many who transracially adopt and those agencies and organizations who transact those adoptions that somehow the native country and culture that the prospective transracial adoptee heralds from is inferior. I would say that it is an institutionalized misconception, akin to the institutionalized and structural racism that Western society is still very much prone to.

Back in late seventies and early eighties, I returned to the country of my birth, Hong Kong. I did this on my own. I traveled to Hong Kong as I left it, alone and unsupported. I saw little point in informing my adoptive parents about my trip as this would only have caused further discord and suspicion about my motivation for such a journey. At the time of going to Hong Kong I did not have the mental strength or the courage needed to visit the orphanage, where I spent the first eleven months of my life. Deep down I was afraid of what I would not find. So rather than face my loss, which at the time I did not fully understand I choose to avoid it completely.

I believe many transracial adoptees grow into the problems that were seeded by their transracial adoption and nourished by the lack of support and understanding that they failed to receive from their adoptive family and parents. These are complex, interconnected and interlocking issues, the roots of which are deep and touch upon the very nature of our being - of who and what we are and how we interface with the society we live in. By being culturally, racially and linguistically displaced a perfect identity storm is waiting to come into creation. It does not have to, but I would say more times than not it is. It sits in the background waiting, for the many triggers and potential challenges maturity and adulthood will bring - the major life markers like getting married or partnered, setting up your first home, giving birth to your first child. All these momentous and usually joyous occurrences can be a deadly double-edged sword.

As a transracial adoptee you lose everything. The building blocks that place you as a person in society, your cultural, racial and heraldic foundations have been removed. The DNA of your identity, something the majority of people take for granted, has been erased. All the component parts that secure and connect a person to their immediate environment and the societies in which they grow up in have been removed, severed, erased. For the transracial adoptee, it is not just the loss of their family, as if that were not enough, but everything and anything that gives a human being context. We lose the ability to communicate in our mother tongue. We have been amputated from our ancestry, history, culture, racial and ethnic lineage. A transracial adoptee fights every moment of their young lives (whether they understand that or not) to find their place in this new environment, to which they have been grafted onto. There is a constant pull between the life a transracial adoptee is being groomed into and the reality of not only the life that the child was taken from, but the life that the adult can expect. The wider society, into which the transracial adoptee grows up in does not suffer these children willingly. The adopting parents' aspirations seldom meet with the practicalities and societal mindset of the host nation. In other words transracial adoptees are raised into the world of white privileges that they themselves will never be able to benefit from.

I was raised in such a manner in the midst of a white community with all the inherent and inbuilt expectations of white privilege. However, as a person of color I was never ever going to be able to take advantage of my upbringing, because I was never ever going to grow up to be a white person. As a child, teenager and young adult this was very confusing and frustrating to say the least. This drove the need in me to recover what information and knowledge I could about my past so that I would be able to better grasp the whys and hows and make some sense of how I fit into the society that relinquished me and the society that raised me. This journey for knowledge that I embarked upon later in life as an adult finally enabled me to build a degree of internal stability in my life.

So helping an adopted child in their search is imperative; it is in my view essential for the child's emotional and personal development and stability. It will likely be one of the most difficult, demanding things that an adoptive parent has to undertake because it demands absolute selfless, non-egotistical, no-blame, no transference of adult sensibilities or emotions. It requires the adoptive parent to divest themselves of any self-motivated preconceptions. It demands that the adoptive parent be so grounded and self-assured, to be themselves deeply rooted and unshakably secure of their own identity, so grounded, that they will not be phased, hurt, or mistake the adoptive child's need to understand as a rejection of the adoptive parents (which it is not). I have encountered many prospective adoptive parents and adoptive parents, that have turned their child's questions and search for their birth family members into an act that is hurtful to them, turning their child's need into actions that affect the adoptive parent, into actions that make the adoptive parent the center of the universe. Twisting a child's natural inquisitiveness in to something that has harmed the adoptive parent, that has made them feel uncomfortable, threatened, unloved, betrayed and in some extreme situations hated. Many adoptive parents find dealing with questions about race and culture extremely difficult. In general (and this is a broad generalization) I have found that the adoptive parents have never considered the matter of race or ethnicity. They have (naively) thought that love and a good home (in material and financial terms) is going to be enough. If only it were that simple.

Transracially adopting a child puts the adopting parents immediately on the back foot without them realizing it. The majority of transracially adopting parents are white, middle-class, privileged and well educated; they have no direct experience of the specific racially orientated challenges and obstacles their transracially adopted child will face throughout his or her life, whether that is in practical matters from personal grooming, lactose intolerance, and skin conditions (experienced by many East Asians because of a change in climate) or overt and covert prejudice and racism. Many adoptive parents that I have encountered in the UK are grossly ignorant and untrained in these matters. They have little to no understanding of the politics of race or diversity in their own immediate environments—let alone from further afield. These parents have never had to worry about the color of their skin or their place in society.

The family into which I was adopted, I think it is safe to say, was a typical, low to mid-middle class, White British family. Times being what they were and the attitudes of the day on race, ethnicity, diversity, and the non-acceptance of color in 50s and 60s Britain of course played a huge part in how I was raised. Anyone in Britain who was not white stood out like a sore thumb and was subjected to overt prejudice and racism. People of color, at that time, were considered as "other" outside the norms of White British society and therefore the perceptions of Black and East Asian inhabitants came from a place of ignorance, fear, and centuries of miss-information fed by racist misconceptions, stereotypes, and racial tropes. I was surrounded by people who bore no resemblance to me, or I to them. When I watched television I rarely saw people who looked like me. When I did they were bad people, they were evil and untrustworthy and spoke English with a very peculiar accent. Of course I later learnt that many of these "Chinese" people that I saw in films or TV dramas, were not actually Chinese; they were white actors pretending to be Chinese.

My search for my birth family would have been a way to try and reconnect to my birthright and my cultural inheritance. It would have been a way of trying to claw back what everyone else around me had - roots, history, and lineage - but I was never allowed to do this. Had I been supported as a child and teenager certain aspects of my life would have been very different and far more positive than the actuality. I recently heard one pair of adoptive parents say the following, "We've adopted a child, opened our home, our lives, our family to that child. We've allowed that child to become a part of our family. That's more than enough. Why would they need to go searching for things that they left behind that?"

As an adoptive parent you have to do all of the above - and more. Just because your transracially adopted child now has a new home, it is not a good enough reason to ignore their previous one, however humble. By ignoring their previous existence you are invalidating and devaluing that life, the country, culture, and the people in it, and by extension your child as a person.

I received no support whatsoever with regard to being taught about my culture, language, or racial and ethnical heritage. If anything I was actively discouraged from asking questions. I do acknowledge it was a different time and a very different place to the multicultural, poly ethnic, and diverse Britain of the 21st century. The picture that was painted of East Asia and Communist China was heavily influenced by the fear of the cold war and the ignorance of the West of China and socialist ideologies. The lack of support or encouragement when I was growing up was driven predominantly by my adoptive parental denial, ignorance, and subliminal arrogance that the West is best.

We know so much more about psychology, about the importance of identity and the perceptions of identity, both individual and communal. We also understand the importance of culture and how that plays an integral and vital part in individual development. I was not supported racially, culturally, or linguistically, so I simply did not bother to go there. I probably missed valuable and viable opportunities during the 70s to find living members of my birth family. Time has marched on, and any remaining blood relatives that might have been willing to come forward with information are probably dead. I will never, in all likelihood, ever be reunited with my birth family. I will probably never be able to discover the true nature of my cultural inheritance and exactly where I came from, other than the fact that I was born (it is assumed) in Hong Kong and abandoned on a public stairwell in Kowloon.

It is of vital importance that as soon as an adoptee starts asking questions about their roots or searching for biological relatives that the response they receive from their adoptive parents is both positive and supportive. The adoptive parents and adoptee can embark upon this journey together, assuming that the adoptee wants this. Why is it that many adoptive parents take offense when an adoptee wants to go it alone? Do not take offense if the adoptee does not initially want company on their journey. It is their journey; **it is not about you**, so stop pulling focus and making it about you. After all, it is an intensely personal and private matter. I have encountered many adoptive parents who react with indignation, in some cases almost righteous anger, with feelings of betrayal and rejection because their transracially adopted child has the temerity to want to know where and who they come from. How dare their adopted child behave in this manner! How dare this child show such disdain and lack of gratitude! Children, no matter how they come into the world and join families, are not possessions. In my personal opinion, it is not a human right to have a child. It is a privilege and a responsibility, that many of us, as untested first-time parents, can never quite conceive of at the beginning of the parental Odyssey. Transracially adopted children are like any other children - just children, who seek to make some sense of the world about them and how they fit into that world.

As a parent you are expected to hover in that background ready and waiting to pick up the pieces if need be. Because as parents isn't that what we have to do? As adoptive parents your job is slightly more complicated. You have a child with history. Maybe they do not know anything about that history yet. They will have baggage, much of which is hidden, initially, all of which, you as a parent will have to help your child unpack, sort, wash, iron, and put away. Your child at some point will want to know 'where did I come from and why am I here'. Some children or teenagers will want to go all the way to the terminus of their adoption journey. Others will disembark only a few stops down the line. Some will not even get past the ticket office, but that is up to them. It is up to the adoptee to decide when and how far they travel on their journey of discovery and personal reclamation.

It is not up to the adoptive parents to dissuade, block, or otherwise hinder that search. The adoptive parents need to help facilitate any such search to make sure that when their child, teenager, or adult child comes out with those questions that they are ready, willing, and able to help that adoptee put the missing pieces of their puzzle together. Adoptive parents that discourage, deny, and prohibit the adoptee from finding out about their past only create problems for themselves and their children. These problems might not manifest themselves for decades, but the seeds of emotional turmoil and discord have been sown.

It took me many years of therapy to reconcile the act of being transracially adopted to who and what I am, to be comfortable with that person, and to come to terms with being a person of color and difference who was shoe-horned into a culturally white dominant society. In the UK, even in the 21st century, it is still hard for the wider society to accept a person of color like me. With the persistence of institutionalized, structural racism and prejudice towards East Asians in the UK, I am part of a minority which is at the bottom of the pecking order amongst other British minorities.

Life for a person of color who has been culturally dislocated and disenfranchised is hard enough; do not add to that burden by actions that are less than supportive of an adoptee's search for their roots. Whether I had been supported at an early age or not is unlikely to have changed the outcome that I will never know who my birth parents are or whether I have relatives or siblings still living in Hong Kong or mainland China. I will never know the reason why my parents relinquished me, but had I had the support of my adoptive parents I think I would have been spared the many dark nights and years of internal mental torment. I might have "found" and made peace with myself decades earlier.

As Philip Larkin wrote in his now infamous poem "This Be The Verse"

They f**k you up, your mum and dad.

They may not mean to, but they do.
They fill you with the faults they had
And add some extra, just for you.

People often misconstrue the idea of support. Support does not necessarily mean you have to agree with the actions of another, but in spite of your own personal feelings you are still there for that person. That is what support means, and adoptive parents have to do for their children. Like any parent, an adoptive parent is there to pick up the pieces in the same way that a parent is there ready with the band aids and antiseptic cream.

As an adoptee I would have given anything to have had a grown up supporting me or at least be there for me, someone that I trusted with life experience that I could talk to. Someone who could help contextualize my fragmented life story. I did not have that. There was no one there that could fulfill that role. I say this not because I want sympathy but to raise awareness for the adoptive parent. Just because you do not have to worry about your heritage, where you come from, your social, cultural, or racial identity does not mean that your transracially adopted child will not have questions or face challenges. They may not; they might have a circle of friends in whom they can confide, from which they can gain an understanding of their difference. Identity, belonging, and race do matter, in spite of what some childcare organizations might say. When it comes to being a child of difference, a child of color, it matters.

Adoptive parents who shut out and try to deny that their child had a life before they were adopted are denying their child an integral part of their existence. My adoptive parents did this because they were ignorant of other cultures, because in the 50s and 60s attitudes to race and other cultures was very different than they are today, because they were instructed to apply the "clean break" approach and sever all ties with the child's past and move on. That does not work, and we now know so much more about how we form our own identity. Do not turn your back on the very things that make your child unique and special. Help your child to grow into a fully rounded and grounded human being, who understands where they have come from, who appreciates the duality of their roots and who can walk forward, knowing that the label transracial adoptee or person of color will not define or confine them, because they truly know and understand where they have come from and how they fit into the world that surrounds them.

I suppose the one advantage of searching later on in life is that you have the maturity and life experience (one hopes) to cope with what the search might uncover. For me it was the disappointment that before I ever really got started my search was over. The orphanage that I spent my first eleven months in was demolished in the early 90s and the records that they held were destroyed (that fact I do find very odd). The records that were kept are not very substantive or informative. I know where I was abandoned, my approximate age, and that is about it. With the inroads into DNA screening I might go down that route – but it would likely only broadly tell me my genetic connections.

Do not let your child be another me, where it takes them the best part of thirty adult years to understand and begin to unravel who and what they are and where they fit in.

As an adoptive parent if you have the opportunity to help your child find those genetic, historic, racial and cultural connections, then embrace it.

REFERENCE

Feast, J.; Grant, M., Rushton, A.; Simmonds, J.; & Sampeys, C. (2013). *Adversity, Adoption, and Afterwards: A mid-life follow-up study of women adopted from Hong Kong.* London, UK: British Association for Adoption and Fostering (BAAF).

It's My Search, Not My Adoptive Parents'

Deanna Doss Shrodes

Deanna Shrodes is the Women's Ministries Director for the Pen-Florida District of the Assemblies of God. She is an ordained Assemblies of God minister and served for twenty-eight-years as co-pastor alongside her husband, Larry who is lead pastor of Celebration Church Tampa (AG). She is a speaker in demand in the United States and abroad, an accomplished musician, worship leader, songwriter and certified coach. Deanna is an award winning writer and contributing author of five highly acclaimed anthologies and sole author of the books, *Juggle: Manage Your Time, Change Your Life; Worthy to Be Found*; and *Restored*, all published by Entourage Publishing. She has been featured in many publications worldwide, including *The Huffington Post*.

* * *

"If he ever wants to search, I have told him we will do it together," said a friend of mine who is an adoptive mom. She was referring to her son, and a possible search and reunion as he grows to adulthood. I wanted to scream, but I didn't. Adult adoptees have to learn to control ourselves in these types of social interactions or it can really affect our relationships, our job, and more.

My friend made this declaration right after she confided to a group of friends that she really hoped her son would never want to search. I wanted to scream at that too, but contained myself. Sitting with a blank stare on my face, the thought I had was, if you really don't want him to search and yet you have told him you will do it together if he ever wants to, it is clear you just want to control the process should he pursue it.

I am sensitive to this type of behavior because I have experienced first-hand what it is like to have an adoptive parent who wanted to control the process. It is not fun. In fact, it is one of the hardest things I have had to deal with as an adoptee. I was an adult living away from home when I got serious about searching, but along the way, my adoptive mother would ask me all about the search, hungry for details. I did not want to share the details with her, preferring to talk to my husband or those who were helping me in the actual search. My adoptive mother is extremely emotional, sensitive, and prone to hurt feelings. I felt as if I had to walk on eggshells as I searched or revealed information, so she would not break down crying about how my findings affected her. When I entered reunion, her interjections in the process reared up at every turn.

Angela Tucker's documentary, *Closure*, was an insightful journey to watch. As I did, one thing that stood out to me was that all adoptees definitely do not feel the same way about search and reunion. Angela's parents were with her every step of the way, and she seemed to desire it. Her family traveled all over the place in the fifteen passenger van, searching for her birth parents. Everyone could see by the footage how close a family they are. I thoroughly enjoyed viewing Angela's heartwarming experience, and yet, my experience is radically different. I am sure part of that is because the relationship every adoptee has with their parents is unique. My adoptive mother and I have struggled, and I have always felt from her a strong desire to possess or control me. Add to this her penchant for secrets and it was an environment for a perfect storm.

From the beginning I had a fear my adoptive mother would try to take over my reunion or develop a relationship with my birth mother without my involvement. Truthfully it was my worst nightmare. I wanted the freedom to develop the relationship with my birth mom without any interference. Unfortunately, my fears were not unfounded. Within days of reunion, Judy (my birth mom) confided to me that she got a letter in the mail from my adoptive mother. The communication was several pages long and indicated her desire that they develop a relationship. For some adoptees their two moms becoming close friends would be a dream; it was my worst fear. Again, I wanted to scream! But I was afraid I would scare my birth mom away, so I didn't.

Rather than letting me set the terms of the reunion, my adoptive mother acted on her own. I was so angry. A part of me wanted to ask Judy not to answer her letter, but I did not want to be controlling. I said nothing, and prayed with all my might that she would not answer it. Judy and I did not know each other well, and I had no idea what she would do. I was overwhelmingly relieved when she told me of her own accord that she would not be answering my adoptive mom's letter. In the years to come it would bother me that Judy was not a deep connector or someone to respond to such invitations from me or really from anyone that I could ascertain. Ironically, this was a gift when it came to my adoptive mother. When Judy let me know she found the letter to be strange and had no intentions of answering it, I breathed the biggest sigh of relief ever. Our relationship was complicated enough and the rollercoaster of reunion so intense that if my adoptive mother were inserted in the middle of our challenges I probably would have needed a lot more therapy than I have already had.

As I talk to other adoptees, I meet many who relate the same story of their adoptive mother writing a letter to their birth mother. And nobody who has ever talked to me was happy about it! I have often quipped, "Do they all go to the same school to learn this stuff?" What gives the adoptive mothers the idea to write such letters? Do they read about other people doing it, or is it their instinctive drive to secure their position? I am not sure. **But it's not about them.** I am the one who was adopted. It happened to me. Everyone else made the choices years ago on my behalf. But now I am grown. I have a mind of my own. I can make my own decisions. And now this is MY reunion.

It is not a process to be dictated by my birth parents or my adoptive parents. I can speak for myself now and manage my relationship on my own without their help. Any talk by all of my parents behind my back feels too much like childhood. Birth and adoptive parents call all the shots until the adoptee is an adult, and finally in adulthood the adoptee should be in the driver's seat. We should get to set the terms of reunion.

Undoubtedly some adoptees will believe I am the crazy one. They would consider it a dream for their adoptive or birth parents to chart the course of the reunion or carry on behind the scenes independently of them. But I find far more adoptees who seem to feel the way I do. It is rather bizarre when sixty-year-old parents are still trying to insert themselves in the decisions of their forty-year-old son or daughter.

And really, it bothers me when friends with underage adopted children tell me it is what they are going to do. I want to say what makes you believe he will tell you all the details of his search or reunion? Do you feel entitled to all of the information as he discovers it? Do you want to be there to control the narrative as much as possible or is this really about supporting him? Is this more about solidifying your position or encouraging your son?

I say none of that because most adoptive parents – even close friends of mine – just do not get it. They so often believe they are entitled to walk through the search and reunion, have the details in real time, and be the first ones who are called and informed at every turn. It is one reason why I have too many friends to count who are actually in reunion and their adoptive parents do not even know it! Or, they waited until their adoptive parents died to search and reunite. They take the chance and some of them find a grave instead of a person. They wait partly out of what is known as adoptee loyalty but also because they are convinced their parents would try to control the process and their reunion would be messed up.

I have also learned first-hand that adoptive parents will sometimes ask others whom their son or daughter are close to in an effort to find out information about their search and reunion. My younger (adopted) sister is currently searching. I have been asked for details. When anyone, including my adoptive parents ask me, my response is, "Whatever she may want to share with you, she will do so personally." This is her search, not our parents', not mine, or anyone else's but hers. For that matter, although I am a fellow adoptee, I do not pry concerning her search. Whatever she wants to tell me, she will. She's a big girl.

Sometimes I just want to scream to the world, "Darn it, adoptive parents! Loose that search and reunion and let it go!!! It's not yours!!" But I don't. Relationships. Jobs. Fitting into society and all that jazz.

It gets exhausting at times to keep yanking the search and reunion back from others who try to control it. Thankfully the adoptee community is there to rely on when I need to scream about wrestling to keep my search and reunion mine and just cannot hold it in any more. I even called on the adoptee community to help with this chapter. I asked, "How can adoptive parents' involvement hinder a search/reunion relationship? And how can adoptive parents be appropriately supportive if their son or daughter is searching?" And here is a sampling of what they shared with me. All names have been changed to allow adoptees to speak candidly without fear of consequences.

"Adoptive parents need to realize, **it is not about them**. It is about us trying to make sense of who we are. It would be great if they could go elsewhere to get the support they need with their insecurities so they could be free and strong enough to offer emotional support without wanting or needing to control. My first mother came to look for me by writing to my adoptive mother. I ended up comforting my adoptive mother as well as my first mother when she showed up. What I really needed was a parent who could be present with what I needed and help me with the waves of emotional turmoil I was experiencing. Selfish of me to want that maybe, but I was their adult child and needed their support more than at any other time.

Angelina—I did an intermediary search in the late 90's. My birth mother was located and she wanted nothing to do with me. I never spoke to her, never heard from her, not even with my medical background. She told the intermediary she wanted no contact and that was that. My adoptive parents were AWESOME. They listened to me whenever I needed to talk. They encouraged me in my search to begin with. They were outraged along with me when I needed them to be; they comforted me when I needed it. They were the rational voice when I could hear it. There are WONDERFUL adoptive parents are out there.

Mary Beth—Some adoptees wait for adoptive parents to pass away so as to avoid them being upset that their son or daughter has reunited with their natural parents. This is a ludicrous situation and adoptive parents need to realize that their child will not abandon them just because they meet their natural parent/s. If the relationship was strong to begin with, it will remain strong.

Marc—Do not make the ADULT adoptee feel guilty for searching, at all. Do not speak ill of the birth parents to the adoptee. An adoptee has every right, need, and desire to find where 100% of their genetics were derived. No one should make someone feel bad for having that desire. My adoptive mom was awesome! My father was a bit unusual. As his own aunt said, he could be insecure and hateful. The only time he heard me ask about my birth parents was to ask of their health history as my ex and I had fertility issues. He said, "What, aren't we good enough for you?" Don't think for a minute that I ever forgot those words, nor the look on my mom's face.

Annette—Adoptive parents: Don't threaten to "disown" your child if they ever decide to search. Don't threaten to "write them out of the will", and when the child or adult does a search and finds a birth parent, don't refuse to meet them. You do have that option but I guarantee it's going to change the relationship you have.

Steve—An adoptive parent can hinder the search by not being supportive of search/reunion. There are several ways of not being supportive, including but not limited to: not giving adoptee necessary information to search, tearing down the biological mother whenever the adoptee asks any questions, closing the door on any talk of adoption unless it's brought up only by the adoptive parent for bragging rights on how they took in and adopted this unwanted child of theirs. That God didn't bless them with any of their own, so they adopted."

Annie—The adoptive parent can be supportive unlike my adoptive mother who always trashed my birth mother whenever I asked any questions. Every time I asked about finding my birth mother my adoptive mother always told me that my birth mother tossed me away like a piece of trash, so why would I want to search. At age 49 I searched on my own, with the support of my husband and grown children. I found my birth mother and three full older siblings. I've been in reunion for 14 years.

Sandie—If my adoptive mother would have been open to my searching, this is what would have been helpful from her: giving me necessary information to help me in my search, asking me how the search was going, offering support of love when obstacles came, sharing in my excitement if reunion occurred and was positive, and offering support if reunion was declined by my birth parent. It would have been meaningful that if hurts were inflicted upon me that she be there to listen and care. And, if reunion went well, to be willing to be part of a new larger family containing both my adoptive and birth family."

Lianna—My adoptive mother did things that were very helpful. She adopted my brother and I through foster care. If I were to list how she was supportive and this started way before my search, I would list these things.

1. She never put down my biological Mom or Dad.

2. She always did her best to answer my questions, even when they must have stung (when I learned about heaven I asked her if when I got there I would recognize my Mom.)

3. She always knew that I wanted to meet my Mom. She neither discouraged or made a big deal of it. She simple let me be.

4. When I was a teenager she brought to me all the records she had and let me see them and have access to those items. At this time she asked me to wait until I was an adult to do the search. I honored that request and it was such a wise decision.

5. She was there when I met my Mom.

Danae—I wish my parents would have truly helped me. My adoptive parents were so upset that I wanted to search. They denied me any Information saying they would tell me everything when I was twenty-one. Well that day came and went. Finally when they did cave in to my requests I was told a last name and given the wrong spelling of that name. That's it. Over twenty years later they still get upset if a say a word about it. I did find my birth mom, without their help.

Cindy—How do adoptive parents hinder a search and reunion? Multiple ways. Lying, guilt trips, refusing to answer reasonable questions, emotional over-reactions (yelling, threatening, crying, ultimatums...) How can adoptive parents be supportive? Do the reverse of the above, be accepting of whatever the adoptee decides.

Alan—Adoptive parents already made their choice, and benefited from, participating in a closed adoption. Let it stay closed for them. Adoptees didn't choose that. It is only fair that adoptees get to choose how to handle everything concerning their adoption once they are adults. Suggestions for AP's include:

* COMPLETE and honest information should be provided to all adoptees, without them having to ask for it, before they reach adulthood. No secrets about anything!

* It's the adoptee's choice when to search, and for whom to search, and at what pace to search.

* It's the adoptee's choice to involve anyone, including adoptive family members, or not. It's called reunion for a reason - the adoptee is reuniting with their own origins. It's not the adopter's family, nor were they ever connected to our natural families.

Search and reunion is already a tremendous drain on an adoptee's time, finances, and emotional resources. Adopters tend to try to make adoptee's reunions about themselves when **it's not about them**, and that's not fair to adoptees to have to meet all those additional emotional needs of the adoptive family at that time.

Sadly, too many adoptive family members, do more harm to an adoptee's reunion than they do to help it. That's why I don't recommend introducing them to an adoptee's natural family until after the adoptee has already securely stabilized those relationships on their own, if they choose to ever involve the adoptive parents at all. The type of support an adoptee most needs during search and reunion seldom comes from an adoptive family. A better source of support would be other adoptees who have been through it.

Janet—As you can see, adoptee opinions and desires run the gamut. My final word on this is that adoptive parents would do well to strip themselves of all hyper-sensitivity and self-serving, and ask the adoptee, "What do you want of me in this matter?" Then, whatever the adoptee says, do that with absolutely no offense, or repercussions. It appears the adoptive parent who can deliver that is rare, but there are a few I have met that give this to their son or daughter. My hope and prayer is for many more.

REFERENCE

Closure. Prod. Bryan A. Tucker. Fob & Dongle Productions LLC., 2013. DVD.

Reunion vs. Relationship

Jodi Haywood

Taken at age two, Jodi grew up in a closed relative adoption and eventually reunited with both parents. Married with a teenage daughter and adult stepdaughter, Jodi has contributed to *Adoption Therapy* (Entourage, 2014), *The Adoptee Survival Guide* (2015), and *Flip the Script* (The AN-YA Project, 2015). Also a fiction writer and a proud member of the Marathon Maniacs running club, Jodi is working toward a bachelor's degree in psychology and qualifying for the Boston Marathon. She plans to continue her studies and work in post-adoption counseling, with a focus on neurological disorders.

* * *

The summer I was twelve-years-old, for about five days, I had a father. I had spent the previous ten years missing him, and after those five brief days were over, I would go back to missing him. I had to leave part of myself behind in order to survive that second separation—the part that allowed myself to have relationships and trust people to stay in my life.

At that time I knew nothing of maternal narcissism. I was not aware of the forces behind the controlling behavior of the woman who had adopted me – my own father's elder sister. I knew that I did not have a close bond with her, that it left a bad taste in my mouth having to call her 'Mom', and that frustration did not begin to describe how I felt when she refused to divulge any information about who or where my "other" parents were. She would tell me when I was older, she kept saying. Until then, I let my imagination fill in all the blanks, mostly about my father.

When she finally did tell me the truth, I had about a month to revise everything I had imagined and rewire my brain to accept that my father and the man I had called "Uncle George" for as long as I could remember were one and the same, to accept that for the last ten years, I had not been living with two genetic strangers, but my only biological aunt and her husband. My aunt had not withheld my story from me because she did not know it, but because she did not want *me* to know it.

For as long as I had been writing to my father as "Uncle George," I had wanted to meet him. I could not explain why. My aunt had moved to another country several years earlier, removing me from my homeland in order to adopt me, so it was not as if I was geographically close to the rest of my family. My father and aunt did not have a close relationship; he did not live down the street or in the next town or even in the next state. I went ten years without seeing him or talking with him on the phone. I do not even remember seeing a decent photo of him, so although I had been adopted by a blood relative, it might as well have been a stranger adoption for all I saw of my biological parents. I had not known my aunt or uncle before going to live with them at about twenty-one-months-old; the adoption was finalized two years later.

I realize the "relative adoption" angle makes my story unique, but even when your aunt adopts you, your birth certificate gets altered to show her as your "mother". When she and your uncle have a different surname, yours gets changed to theirs. Even when you find out they are your aunt and uncle and you are about to reconnect with your dad, they will not let you call them "aunt" or "uncle". You are expected to use the term "uncle" for your father, whom you knew until you were nearly two years old. It never occurs to them that you might find this confusing or unwelcome or downright ridiculous and not want to comply with it.

The fact that my father's sister even wanted to adopt me and change the relationship, at least on paper, is proof of her controlling, narcissistic personality. *She* wanted to be "mom", not just guardian aunt, and she insisted over and over – even as I prepared to reunite with my mother in my mid-twenties – that *she* was my mother. Unable to become a mother the natural way, she used me to compensate for her infertility and perhaps her jealousy over the fact that her brother could parent children while she could not.

GENETICS AND ENVIRONMENT: AN INSEPARABLE COMBINATION?

The scientific debate of nature vs. nurture, heredity vs. environment, has been tossed back and forth for decades. Which one has a more powerful influence over our lives?

The prevailing psychological viewpoint, according to my university textbooks, is that the two are inseparably connected. The type of upbringing we receive and the experiences we go through affect what we do with the physical and psychological traits we inherit from our parents. But for adoptees, at least the way many of us were raised, nature and heredity are denied. Historically, adoptive parents were handed a baby along with the blank-slate mentality: raise it as their own, love it enough, and as long as it grew up healthy and well-adjusted, it would never wonder about or attempt to search for its origins. Nowadays we know the naïveté, even the ignorance of such beliefs.

We have many reasons to want to seek out our origins, our roots, our blood relatives. Maybe our desire is to find someone we physically resemble, since we grew up without that genetic mirroring and have no idea from whom we inherited our eyes, nose, hair, build, etc. Maybe we want to know what we ourselves will look like in twenty or thirty years, since nobody in our adoptive family can give us a glimpse of our future selves. Or maybe it is a need to know our medical history: which illnesses run in the family? Do I require early screening for cancer or diabetes? Do I need to adjust my lifestyle now in order to avoid heart disease later? Is there a history of mental illness or alcoholism? Am I inadvertently risking passing on something to my children?

Sometimes there is a need to establish relationships with our biological family. This is a natural human desire and does not necessarily stem from lack of relationship or dissatisfaction with our adoptive family. Many adult adoptees claim to have close, secure relationships with their adoptive family and still search for their birth parents or other biological relatives. Some manage to maintain close ties with both the original and adoptive families, even merging them into one "extended family." Others meet just once, satisfy their curiosity, and close that door forever.

Most of us are somewhere between those two. Relationships are complex, especially in adoption, when—as is often said—family becomes strangers and strangers become your new family, frequently in the span of one day. This goes against nature. Babies have not only an instinctive connection to their mother, forged during nine months of prenatal bonding, they also have a built-in resistance to strangers. This defense mechanism prevents them from attaching to somebody other than the mother, on whom they depend for nurture, nourishment, and protection. If somebody attempts to hold a baby separate from its mother for any length of time, the baby will become fussy, anxious, and next to impossible to soothe; only Mom will do.

This became clear to me when my daughter was about a week old. My aunt and uncle were visiting, and my aunt encouraged my husband to take me out for a couple of hours for my birthday dinner and some "alone time." When we returned, my aunt informed me our little girl had been "very naughty" and cried the whole time instead of sleeping. How could a six-day-old baby be naughty? Once I took her back, she settled down pretty fast and was asleep in no time. Now, fifteen years later, I have to wonder what I was thinking leaving a week-old baby with an elderly couple who had never had a baby of their own. Keep in mind that I was already 21 months old when my aunt brought me from my homeland to live with them. This same aunt returned to work immediately afterward and left me in the care of a series of babysitters and day homes until I finished fifth grade.

ATTACHMENT STYLES AND COMPLICATIONS

As babies, our very first and most important relationship is with our mother. The one who nurtured us in her womb for thirty-eight-weeks, give or take. Whatever she eats, drinks, or otherwise swallows is passed through the placenta into us, influencing our taste preferences. As newborn babies, we can distinguish her breast milk from that of another woman by scent alone. We know the sound of her voice. We have been part of her, and she is part of us.

When this relationship is broken, it can have a lasting effect on our ability to attach to and build relationships with others, including our adoptive parents. For the first few months of life, a baby is unaware of being a separate entity from the mother. After this phase, the mother is still the center of the baby's world as he or she begins the process of exploring it. The older baby or toddler will display "stranger anxiety", putting up a fight if anybody outside the known family circle attempts to remove them from their familiar environment. The newly adopted toddler who bonds instantly and unquestioningly with his or her adoptive parents is the exception, not the rule.

The effect of breaking the mother/baby or mother/child relationship in such an abrupt and permanent way is devastating. Our earliest and most vital relationship is over, without warning, and no explanation is sufficient to a very young child who has not yet developed logical thinking. A baby does not understand, or care about, the difference between the mother relinquishing due to poverty or ill health and the mother's death. All the baby is aware of is the mother's sudden absence. A replacement mother figure will not reduce anxiety and soothe the baby any more than a fruit-shaped piece of plastic will ease hunger pangs and provide nourishment. In simple terms, this is the wrong mother, and the baby knows it.

Developmental psychologists have conducted much research on the maternal bond and infant attachment. I would recommend starting with Ainsworth et al. (1978) and the "Strange Situation" experiments, in which babies and their mothers or caregivers were placed in a room together for a short time, followed by the arrival of a stranger and then the brief departure of the mother. Ainsworth and her colleagues observed the babies' reactions to the stranger and to their mothers' absence and return; these observations led to the theory of three distinct attachment styles. Securely attached children showed distress in the absence of their mother, but were quickly and easily soothed upon her return. Insecurely attached children fell into one of two categories: *anxious/ambivalent*, those who displayed anxiety while separated from their mothers but remained fretful, distressed and clingy for some time after she came back; and *avoidant*, children who appeared unconcerned about whether their mother was absent or present, neither crying when she left nor seeking contact when she came back; some actually resisted contact. More recent studies indicate that our earliest attachment patterns stay with us for life (cited by Berk, 2012), possibly due to family dynamics remaining fairly constant during our childhood and adolescence. Attachment styles seem to evolve from both personality traits and type of caregiving received.

Some adoptees form secure attachments to their adoptive parents; others do not. With those who do, some take much longer than others. It is impossible to predict which adoptees fall into which category, and many factors are at work. How good of a "fit" is the adoptive family? What is the overall mental health of the child? How resilient is the child? Several prenatal influences can have an adverse effect on the developing brain, on neural activity, and when some congenital brain damage is present, the baby may be less resilient or adaptive to change.

Relationships are based on one foundation above all: trust. When that trust is shattered, it can be extremely difficult to rebuild or restored; the relationship is often irreversibly altered. Nancy Verrier uses the "broken plate" analogy in her book *The Primal Wound* (1994): the mother/child relationship is likened to a plate, broken and then glued back together. Even the best gluing job cannot account for the tiny fragments that could not be reincorporated into the whole. It can be mended, but never completely healed.

In reunion, we are always missing some pieces, and the longer we take to reunite, the more pieces will always be missing. Both sides have missed milestones in each other's lives. In many cases there are siblings we have grown up without, and vice versa. It takes more than just one reunion meeting to catch up on everything, and sometimes, more than one meeting to decide that we even want to.

ADOPTION: A RELATIONSHIP THAT BEGINS WITH A BETRAYAL

Relationships for many adoptees are extremely complicated. We might not be fully aware that our reluctance to place our trust in others is connected to the trust our natural mothers broke when they relinquished us for adoption or possibly to the trust our adoptive parents broke when we discovered we were adopted. For late-discovery adoptees, this can come at any time, during our teen years when the adoptive parents decide we are finally "old enough to know", during our childbearing years when they admit we will not pass on their hereditary diseases to our offspring, the day we apply for a passport and find out our amended "birth" certificate is lacking vital information and not an officially recognized document, or even after their deaths, when we discover the papers from the agency stuck away in their filing cabinet or a safe-deposit box.

Some adoptees are capable of long-term relationships, while others seem to set themselves up for failure again and again, afraid to commit and not completely understanding why. If the first lesson we learn from our mothers is the impermanence of relationship, this may carry over into every aspect of our lives. Friends come and go. Boyfriends or girlfriends do something to break our trust, and we decide to cut all ties rather than give them another chance to hurt us. Or we might decide not to give anybody that opportunity in the first place. Relationships do not last. There is no such thing as "forever". People will only let you down, so you do not get involved.

For the birth mother, one thing to keep in mind prior to reunion is that you have no idea what your son or daughter's adoptive parents have told him or her about you, and sadly, no control over it. It is hard to ask, but if at all possible, try to find out so that you can help them separate truth from lies or speculations. You do not want to overwhelm them with too much information, either. Reunion is an ongoing process, a combination of rebuilding trust and processing information which may be contradictory to the story the adoptee grew up with.

For myself, my adopting aunt did everything wrong. When adopting within one's own family, there must always be an awareness that the adoptee has access to one or more people who know the truth. Another dynamic that may be unique to kinship adoption is that the adoptee, especially as a child, assumes that the biological mother knows exactly where he or she is and how to find him or her, and thus the lack of contact is *entirely* the choice of the mother. "Of course she knows where I am; how could she not?" For a mother not to know the whereabouts of her own child – adopted out or not – is unfathomable. To a young child, mothers are all-knowing - just try to get away with anything behind your adoptive mother's back - so the logical assumption is *she knows where I am, she has never contacted me, therefore, she wants nothing to do with me.*

An incident from my teenage years stands out in detail. I was sixteen that summer when my aunt adopter received a letter from my father which she shared with me. My mother had visited him, suddenly out of the blue, and enlisted his help in locating her two older children – my half-siblings from a previous marriage, whose father had kept them. Dad helped her search, but they never located either of them. Dad said he gave her one of my school photos before she left. I forget what I said to my aunt, but her response was "you're not lost to her". By this time I had several mixed feelings about my mother, but I figured if she had gone to the trouble of trying to locate her other kids, she might want to find me too. I waited for the rest of the summer - no letter, not a word. I decided she wanted nothing to do with me, and my mixed feelings solidified into a mass of anger and resentment at being abandoned once more.

Some of the anger was directed at my aunt adopter. I resented her taking me away from my father, my home, and my extended family in England. Had I still been with my dad, I would have seen my mother when she came back. What I did not know at the time, and would not discover until after my aunt died twenty-years later, was that my mother wanted an ongoing relationship with me. When I was three she wrote to my aunt and asked her to return me to her, or at least allow me to visit, and then decide who I wanted to live with when I was older. I do not have my aunt's reply, but I can guess she refused her request. All those times I missed my mother growing up, all those times I wondered what was wrong with me that caused her not to want me, all of that was my aunt deliberately keeping me apart from her. I did not know this when I first reunited with her, ten years after my dad wrote that letter.

When children grow up in an atmosphere of openness and trust, of freedom to speak their minds and share their fears and concerns, they develop good relationship skills. In homes where adoption is the elephant in the living room, on the other hand, children become an often-unwilling partner in the conspiracy to keep it secret. Adoptive parents can, actively or passively, discourage the child from voicing his or her feelings about being adopted along with any questions about the biological family. The message is clear. *Your voice does not matter, your feelings do not matter, and whoever you were prior to our adoption of you matters least of all.*

This is not a healthy foundation for any relationship. Some adoptees take an attitude of passivity, allowing others to speak, think, and feel for them, out of fear they will be rejected or shunned if they express dissenting views. Others vent their anger on any convenient target. Blame may be placed upon the adoptive parents for taking them away from their biological family; the birth mother may be judged at fault for rejecting them, giving them away to a couple who did not understand them or accept them unconditionally. I am not saying that every adoptee lacks healthy relationship skills. My opinion is that the traumatic events of relinquishment and adoption can have varying adverse effects upon our ability to establish and maintain close relationships, especially when conflict arises.

REUNION OR RELATIONSHIP: WHICH DO I WANT?

Sometimes it helps to ask yourself before you begin your search: what do I want out of this reunion? Where do I want it to lead? Do I want a quick meeting, a "hello, I'm still alive, and now that I have seen the woman who gave birth to me, I can get on with my life"? Do I want a second meeting later on to ask the questions I did not think of the first time around? Do I want an ongoing relationship? Do I want my birth mother to make up for the selfish, narcissistic one who adopted me and set unrealistically high standards, and love me the way my adoptive family never could? Or do I feel as if I would betray my adoptive mother for daring to call another woman "mom"? Do I want to keep the relationship secret until my adoptive parents die? Do I even want to delay beginning my search until they're dead, despite the odds of finding graves instead of parents?

This is a good idea, in theory, even if the reunion pans out in ways you had not planned or anticipated. Reunion, after all, takes two people – at least two. You may hit it off immediately, spend hours discovering all the things you have in common, or your first mother may have a husband and other children who do not know you exist and is afraid it would be too awkward to continue a relationship although you desperately want one. But it is still a good exercise to write down the things you hope to achieve from reuniting with one or both of your birth parents for one simple reason…

Adoptees are very seldom asked what *we* want. The act of adoption is one we are not allowed to participate in. In most instances we are too young to read, let alone comprehend the ramifications of the legal documents. We do not get to choose whether to go home with strangers from the hospital we were born in. We do not get to decide what to call these people who have suddenly replaced our parents. We do not get the freedom to ask about our birth parents or our origins; our questions are met with everything from silence to hurt and guilt trips (*aren't we good enough for you?*) to shaming (*don't you know how much you upset us by bringing* her *up?*) to belittling (*we will tell you when you're more mature.*) If we find out what our name was at birth, we are not allowed to use it. Since the societal expectation of adoptees, even adults, is gratitude that we were rescued from abortion or poverty or some other horrific circumstances, we usually are not asked how we feel about it.

Not everybody has control freaks for adoptive parents, but narcissism seems to have more impact coming from an adoptive mother than a biological one. It is one thing to have a mother try to mold her flesh and blood into a "Mini-Me" when they share some biological traits. When the child's DNA is entirely separate, those differences are treated as if nonexistent; we are, after all, "as if born to."

It did not hit me until very recently that my aunt adopter controlled nearly every aspect of my life. I was not allowed to choose any of my own clothes until I was 13, and even after that, she would ridicule my choices and continue to buy me clothing more suited to her style and personality than mine - of course, she was old enough to be my grandmother. Eventually all the clothes she selected found their way into her closet. When I was 11, she had my hair cut short, in a style she chose and instructed the hairdresser on. I hated it, almost as much as I hated being mistaken for a boy (it was *that* short.) When I was 12, she decided to redecorate my bedroom, choosing everything from the carpet (pink) to the wallpaper (pink floral), never asking my opinion, never bringing home samples for my approval, never seeking my input. At any time during my childhood I would have given my right arm for a dog or even a cat, but she did not allow me any pets, nothing to fill the void of the siblings I had lost or the friends I had trouble finding.

Going back further, from my 6th birthday on, she took me to several child experts, psychologists, and at least one psychiatrist to try and figure out what was wrong with me. I was about 7½ when one professional suggested to her that my early childhood upheaval and adoption could be one contributing factor in my behavioral problems; she told him point blank that this would be my last session with him. He tried to convince her I would benefit from ongoing therapy, but her mind was made up and I did not see him again, at least, not until I was 11 and my behavior had worsened. But any files from that time period were not among those I found after my aunt's death in 2010. She controlled my appearance, my relationships, my education (I attended schools five miles from our neighborhood in an upper-class area just because they offered "special programs for the disabled." The irony is my high-functioning autism went undiagnosed all through my school years, and if she had not pulled me out of therapy, somebody might have figured it out sooner. My aunt made it all about her, even my reunion with my biological mother.

Whether you are an adoptee or a birth parent preparing for reunion, it is important to take an honest look at your own attachment style and to consider that in adoption secure attachment tends to be the exception and not the rule. The adoptive mother who believes her daughter is securely attached when she stays close to her side, seeks her protection, confides secrets in her, allows matching outfits or hairstyles, and phones or texts her from school or when she is staying at a friend's house is possibly mistaking "secure" attachment for anxious-ambivalent. An overly clingy child may suffer from separation anxiety (extremely common among adoptees) and an equally anxious adoptive mother, fearful of doing the wrong thing, may encourage this type of behavior. A securely attached child has the freedom to develop a healthy and age-appropriate level of independence.

Adoption reunion can be awkward; there is no easy way past that stage. You once shared one of the most intimate relationships any two people can have, that of mother and baby; it is unnatural for a mother and baby to become strangers, regardless of the circumstances. You have missed out on years together, decades. You need to get to know this person in light of the changes and experiences they have gone through during those years. You are not sure if you still have the right to consider yourselves mother and child, in the sense of offspring since you are both adults now (or father and child); in my opinion, you do, but *each individual adoptee is different.* I cannot emphasize that enough.

Another thing you want to try and avoid is over-analyzing (I do that all the time.) For the adoptee especially, everything and everyone gets analyzed. What if I do something wrong? Or later, going over it in your head, what did I do wrong? Any perceived wrong move can lead to the end of a relationship. Some of us have grown up believing it is our job not to disappoint others or let them down, or believing we needed to earn our keep in our adoptive families because we had no actual right to be there. Some of us were the scapegoat in our adoptive families; everything was our fault. If something "goes wrong" in reunion, even if only in our own minds, we tend to blame ourselves. Again, we were not good enough to keep. *It is extremely important to get past this mindset in order to experience healthy relationships as adults.*

Look at the reunion relationship as one you have a lifetime to build, if you choose to. Take a deep breath. Enjoy each other's company. Soak up the novelty of seeing your eyes, your eyebrows, your nose on someone else's face and feel that connection. Hear your laugh from her or him. Watch your mannerisms reflected in them. Let your parent tell you how much you look like an aunt, uncle, cousin, grandparent. Keep in mind how much there is beneath the surface, how much may be different, and remember you do not need to go too deep too fast, unless time is limited for one or both of you. *Adoption reunion is not natural.* It will not be like the relationships you have with your kids, your friends, your spouse, your in-laws, your biological siblings. You are trying to sew back together what was never intended to be torn apart. You might be able to handle a deep level of closeness one day and need to keep the other person at arm's length for some time after that while you process things. Take your time. Needing space is not a rejection.

Start with the reunion. In time, the relationship will come. Do not try and control the direction it goes in, wherever that may be.

REFERENCES

Ainsworth, M.D.; Blehar, S.D.; Waters, E.; & Wall, S. (1978) *Patterns of Attachment.* Hillsdale, NJ: Erlbaum.

Berk, L.E. (2012, 7th ed.) *Infants, Children & Adolescents*, Allyn & Bacon, Boston, MA.

Verrier, N. (1993) *The Primal Wound.* Baltimore, MD: Gateway.

One Birth Father's Story of Reunion

Jeff Chafin

Jeff Chafin was born in Indianapolis, Indiana, in 1966, but relocated to Georgia in 1985 during his senior year of high school. He attended Savannah College of Art and Design. He is currently a freelance graphic designer in the printing business. Growing up with an identical twin brother did not feel like a normal childhood, and they fought to establish their own identities. Jeff eventually tattooed his own finger in sixth grade to help people be able to tell them apart. He was twenty-five when his life took an unexpected change. He reluctantly signed adoption papers knowing that someone would be able to give his daughter more then he could. He married at age thirty-four and had no other children. He is very recently reunited with his daughter and navigating that new relationship.

* * *

The adoption was all a blur to me; my mom had to tell me what happened that day. I had a limited time to decide on my daughter's fate and future. With hesitation and mostly the sadness of knowing I would not be able to care for her, I relinquished my parental rights. I was told only she could do the search, so my search was the waiting and everyday thoughts of where she was or what she was doing, not knowing if she would or would not find me. I was provided the adoption agency's information, so over the years I made contact with them to let them know I was still available, but no replies back or communication came. I made sure that I made things as easy as I could for my daughter to locate me by keeping the same number and living in the same area. I also kept in touch with the first mother, figuring if my daughter did search that she would find her birth mother first. So keeping in touch with the birth mother was vital to me.

My story of reunion is both happy and sad. At first, it was amazing, and in all the excitement I forgot to focus on what is most important - my child. This was mostly due to my sudden surprise and "anxiety" that I am now being held accountable to answer questions and explain a part of my life that I was not sure I wanted to reopen or think about. I did not have a tragic break up or a relationship that was hard with the birthmother; what was more difficult for me was facing these questions on my own. But there was no hesitation for me; I was so excited. I had not had any other children. The reunion I had hoped would come had, but without being prepared for this it has caused some issues for us. Having had so many emotions in the beginning, I believed caused her to pull back and take in everything she had now learned about me, my issues both good and bad. I am seeking help for myself and want so much for her to know that I care about her. It has been difficult for me that she needed to pull back for now because I was not prepared.

Looking back, seeking support groups earlier would have helped me adjust better to meeting my daughter and being able to be as prepared as she was in her search for us. When the day came and I had no idea what was next, I went to look for information or stories related to reunions. My daughter had suggested a group, so I started to go to the meetings. The meetings are held only on the second Tuesday of each month, and I wanted more time and opportunity to work on the questions I had. Searching for as many types of groups and programs I can, I began to realize how little help there is for birth fathers. I am still searching for other groups; there are few of them that I have found so far, but I keep looking. In my researching and going to groups for help I just keep hearing adoptees wanting to know who they are. It is so heartbreaking to me to hear their stories and not want to hug each one of them.

Why are both birth parents important? Wouldn't any child would be curious about who they are at some point in their lives, where they came from, and who they are made up of? It is just as important as it is for a child born into a family that wants to know their history, who their ancestors were, and where their family came from. They teach these things in school. They often ask children to make a family tree for instance. How would you feel if you were asked to show a family tree knowing the roots of the tree are missing? The tree is not a tree without its roots. To think that it was not important is unthinkable.

My daughter wanted all the information she could find to understand what her family tree really was. She told me about making a family tree in the past, and that it had made her always think about where she fit in.

To not have that information in their lives would leave them with questions about themselves and their reason for being who they are. When we met, my daughter told me a story about when she was five; she looked up at her dad and asked why did she feel like she had a hole in her heart. That is when they explained to her what it meant to be adopted, and that began her curiosity about who we (her birth parents) were. There was a missing part of her. The only way to put that puzzle together in full was to find these two middle pieces. She had four corners of the puzzle already. She had a life with her adopted parents and siblings, but those two pieces were also important.

As adoptees grow older, the question will become more curious for them. I was amazed how happy my daughter was to be able to fill out her family history on medical forms. The joy was obvious when she told me about it. There are so many things she wanted to know, and she wanted most of all it seemed to want to find a connection. For the two of us, the connection was the way we are wired, the way we think about things, more of a mental connection, but it was like we had known each other forever. She did not connect as much with her first mother, so it was very important to her to find this connection with me.

Even if the reconnecting turns out to not be a joyful one or the relationship does not evolve, it is still important that they know their answers for their life to grow as full as possible. They are raised in the adoptive family they have become a part of that family; those bonds will be just as strong towards the ones that love them. The emotion to protect them and make sure they are safe will be strong for everyone involved with the process. It is understandable for all adoptive parents to want to protect the child that they have raised and cared for. This is not a contest of who loves who more; it is helping the adoptee understand the questions they have asked themselves from the time they learned about adoption.

Is it fair for a child to not know these things that make them who they are? Are birth parents only a vessel for you to experience happiness in raising a child? Is it your choice now for them to decide if they should know or not? Of course there will be some instances where the birth mother or birth father may not be a good match or create a good environment, but please allow for our children to be able to make contact by mail and at least acknowledge them.

I have to understand each day what my role is as a birth father. I search for answers every day. As birth parents it is our responsibility to understand our place within the circle. We should be understanding when our children need time to process it all at their own speed. I think it is beneficial for both birth and adoptive parents to seek groups of people with similar experiences and discuss it, keep open conversation on these topics to understand the process better for all involved. If we all can work together and help everyone involved I think that everyone would benefit. Allowing adopted children to understand earlier may give them something to believe in and know they are a part of something. The unfortunate part is that while all parents love their children, some may or may not show it or be open to feeling it. For the ones who are open for discussion or to be able to be in a open adoption. It is for the child.

I personally see my daughter's adoptive parents as angels for caring for and protecting my child. When I met them, the first thing I did was hug them. I owe them so much I could never repay them. They protected and cared for her, and gave her an option in life I could not have provided. For that I will always be grateful for them. It hurts to think that possibly adoptive parents feel we are a threat to your family circle. We are grateful for you, yet what we feel is guilt and shame that we could not do what you did.

Visiting these support groups, I find that the adult adoptees are so informed about their emotions and aware of things; I am amazed that in their twenties, they are so focused on something and determined to find answers. They are focused on finding the answers they are missing. Since my experience was being a part of a closed adoption with no contact, I can only believe that open adoption would help overcome these issues of abandonment so much earlier in life. It is something that I would see as helping the children grow, and to have that connection earlier would cure so many of their fears. It may help us as birth parents feel that we can still help our children and overcome the anxiety and overwhelming questions that we ask ourselves. The biggest hurdle would be to figure out how this would work, but the first step is getting there and opening a dialogue between the parents.

It seems anxiety becomes the main theme in all the stories I hear. We could help this problem by thinking about these common problems, and work on solutions to overcome them. What will be most beneficial for our children as grown adults and help them to function normally? In the people I have met, I see so much potential that has been suppressed by these problems. I don't believe therapy should be the most obvious fix to help them function. By the end we are all in therapy trying to understand all the questions, so lets answer them earlier.

I have learned so much over this process. I was not able to make contact with my child while she was growing up, so I have more catching up to do. I have to learn to process she is an adult now. She is not a child anymore. If I had advice for birth fathers, it would be to prepare for your child to be an adult when you meet. You may want to begin a journal for them sharing what you are thinking, and maybe when the time comes you can share it with them. I never knew who she would be, but I did not prepare myself for an adult.

She has told me that we have answered so many questions she has had about herself. And after the second week she was already so much more confident. She has answered the biggest question in her life. With birth parent information, adoptees can begin to put everything together; now the puzzle is finished, and they can begin to start the new puzzle of the life they choose. We should allow for the children to want to know where they come from. And that includes the birth father. We all need a foundation. As a birth father, I think this role it is just as important as a first mother. For my daughter the connection was more with me then her mother. As important as it is to know the birth mother, it is also just as important to have the father involved as well to help adoptees put together the entire puzzle of who they are and where they came from.

Part II

Open Adoption

One Adoptive Mother's Changing Perspective on Open Adoption

Maris Blechner, M Ed, LCSW

Maris Blechner is a Licensed Clinical Social Worker and educator who has been training and presenting on child welfare topics throughout North America for many years. She is one of the founders of Family Focus Adoption Services, and was its first Executive Director for twenty-six-years. These days she also teaches at the Silberman School of Social Work at Hunter College.

* * *

My husband and I are the parents of two adopted daughters as well as a birth son. In one of the many coincidences of life, our son grew up to marry a woman who had been adopted as a baby, so all of the women in our next generation of nuclear family are adoptees. Our children are now adults with children of their own, and I have worked in the field of adoption for many years, so the concepts and realities of open and closed adoption are not new to me. There is no question that there are widely varying opinions on the topic, and my perspective has certainly modified over the years, as adoptive parents so often grow and change in their thinking in many ways. At the New York State adoption agency that I ran, we learned from a master, one long-term adoptive dad, that you have to have a forty year perspective to be involved in adoption, as a parent or a worker, because that is how long our actions of today will influence a child's life. That is certainly true when it comes to my perspective on open adoption.

Our first daughter was born in Seattle, and we brought her home at five-days-old in a totally closed adoption. It was an incredibly exciting day, but I worried all the way to the airport that somehow her birth mother would find us and take back her baby. Certainly it was irrational but not an uncommon fear. At that time, I was glad that the adoption was closed. I also had no idea that open adoption was not a "yes" or "no," but rather a continuum with many choices. I only really learned that when I began to do adoption work in an agency.

Within the spectrum that is open adoption, some birth parents sign a formal request for a letter and pictures every year after the baby's birthday and may or may not want to meet for the placement; some birth and adoptive families create email addresses where they can exchange pictures and information over the years; some families meet in the park every year at the child's birthday or do something together at a neutral setting during school holidays. There are many variables, and as adoptive parents become more comfortable with the degree of openness, it can change. I think getting used to some openness and losing the fear of losing your child is a slow process.

As our first daughter grew, for the first time I realized the loss in having such a closed adoption. Our daughter developed a skin condition that is familial. I would have loved to have someone in her birth family to talk to, to find out what treatment worked for them. This personal situation has caused me to do a lot of thinking about medical issues. Today, I tell prospective and new adoptive parents to consider that a more open adoption means that if your child develops a serious disease, perhaps one that requires stem cells or bone marrow, a more open adoption allows you to reach out for help from the birth family.

As our daughter approached adolescence, I tremendously regretted not having asked to meet her birthmother or not even having asked for a picture, either of which I could have done. I would have loved to show our daughter what she was likely to look like, since women so often grow up to look like their mothers. By this point, I was running an adoption agency. What I learned from the lessons of my own life was to make sure that every pregnant woman considering adoption at our agency has filled out an information sheet with the kinds of details that my husband and I did not have with our own adoption. (These included things like height and weight, clothing and bra sizes, and even the age when a birth mother got her period for the first time.)

Many times birth mothers do not want to name the birth father, which is their right in New York State. What we have done at the agency that I ran was to ask a great many questions of every birth mother about the birth father to get as much information as we could for the adoptive family and most importantly the child. Boys and girls both want to know if either of their parents were good at sports or had other special skills. Birth parents are also always willing to let us take pictures to give the adoptive family for their child to have. In addition, the person at the agency who was closest to the birth family writes a letter to the baby for the time when the child becomes interested, explaining how the adoption took place. Of course it should also be noted that today birth families and adoptive families have the opportunity to share photos through their chosen designated email addresses and to remain in ongoing contact.

In showing how and why my perspective continued to change, I have to mention the special event for any parent, our oldest daughter's wedding. That day, after not really having thought about our daughter's birth mother for years, I felt her birth mother's absence tremendously. As my husband and I walked our beautiful daughter down the aisle together, in the Jewish tradition, I thought about how there was another woman, also her mother, somewhere in the world who had no idea that her daughter was getting married that day. If I could have waved a magic wand and brought her to the wedding to be with us, I would have done it. I was genuinely sad at her absence. I distinctly remember later that day, standing on the edge of the dance floor with my sister, telling her how I felt, and we both cried.

I felt the same way again years later, at another major family life-cycle event, when this same daughter had a baby girl who looked just like she had looked when we brought her home. Our son-in-law is not adopted. His mother and I, the two grandmas, found ourselves together with the baby on one of those early days. The other grandma was busy commenting on how much the baby had features of her family (as grandmas often do). I was struck at that moment by how much adopted people in a closed adoption lose when they have children; they have no one to compare their children to. All I could do was provide as many baby pictures of our daughter as I could, to show how the new baby really looked just like her.

I had these same feelings of loss and that same tremendous regret at our closed adoption when our daughter's second daughter was born. This little girl, talented and beautiful, looks nothing like either parent. Clearly she resembles a grandparent or other relative on our daughter's unknown side – and we have no way to know who it is. I feel as though I am missing important family information, and I am only the grandma.

When our son and his wife (who is an adoptee) had their two children, it hit me again about how much information just is not there in an adopted person's life if theirs is a closed adoption. These two children each have wonderful and unique talents. One is incredibly artistic. The other is fascinated by electronics. It is very likely that they each take after someone. I just wish I knew who those people are.

Our second adopted daughter is from Korea, and she came to us from an orphanage at three years and seven months old. She is now an adult, well known in the fashion design world. When she and her husband, who is Caucasian and not adopted, had a daughter, the other side of the family provided a bunch of pictures of my son-in-law as a baby, to show how much the new baby looked like their side. This time I had no baby pictures to show – because our daughter was older when we met and came with only a few pictures from the orphanage, all they provided in those days. What I did do is flood their baby's room with as many pictures as I had that we took of our daughter in the weeks after she arrived – and it was clear that the baby did indeed look way more like our daughter than her husband.

So I have really grown. The older I get, the more I realize that just as we tell older foster children that are being placed for adoption that there is room in their hearts for more than one mother, we should be telling new and prospective adoptive parents that there is room in their own hearts for their children's birth parents as well. I have come to see adoption not as a child joining a new family, but as two families melding together and becoming one bigger family. The best example I could share are the many stories of adoptions that my agency helped effectuate for the children of birth parents dying of AIDS. In many cases, the birth parent's caregiver stepped up to adopt, sometimes at the birth parent's request, and once I know of a lawyer that did. They all needed an agency, and we provided that service, so I got to see the emotional process up close. It was not only a child that a potential adoptive parent wanted to help; it was the adoptive parents who sat with the dying birth parent, who arranged for the burial, who cleaned out an apartment, who sometimes helped the birth parent make a video for the child to have. They truly all became one family. That is the true nature of adoption.

How do I feel today? Blessed by the family that we have been given, but also cheated in a way. My children are settled in life, loved and loving. Although they have chosen not to search, I have come to realize that I would have loved to know their birth families, and I still feel that way. Today I am more than willing to share my children with them. If I had it all to do over, at the very least I would have met their birth families and taken pictures and tried to establish contact for the future. Sometimes I still have a fantasy of all of us meeting and sitting down together. How could I ever thank a birth family adequately for the gift of my children?

These days there are books to read about the success of open adoption, and every prospective family should be encouraged to read them. The internet has made big changes because pregnant women considering adoption often go to the internet to the various sites where interested potential adoptive parents from all over the United States can list themselves with a picture and write up. A birth parent can reach out to a specific listed family, and they can all meet and get to know each other.

There is no question that new potential families are sometimes worried about relationships with a birth family and can see potential pitfalls. The idea of open adoption may require a flexibility that needs time to develop in a family just starting the adoption process. Sometimes extended family, not used to the idea, can be nervous and say things to make the new adoptive family nervous too. There are even those who say that international adoption is "better," because there is no birth family to worry about. From my long term perspective, my answer to that is "baloney." The greater the distance, the greater can be a child's losses. Since every potential adoptive parent has to have a social worker home study, it is really incumbent on the home study worker and the adoption agency or attorney to discuss the concept of open adoption and any worries that a potential family may have.

Nobody is denying that the risk exists of less-than-satisfactory birth family encounters. However, the potential for good, and meeting a child's information needs (if not medical needs), far outweighs any risks, in my opinion. Raising adopted children is a learning experience. Potential adoptive parents should be encouraged to affiliate with adoptive parent support groups and to talk to adoptive parents who have had different types of open adoptions to hear what they have to say.

I have said for years that adoptive parents have to be a lot smarter than their next-door neighbors, raising what a co-worker used to call "plain old birth kids." Our lives are more complex, more interesting, and in many respects deeper. We have to look at many topics directly, and it is healthy to talk and read and learn about new ideas. Open adoption used to be a new idea; now it is a more and more common practice.

The most important thing an adoptive parent needs to know is what the title of this book says: **open adoption is really not about you**. Our children deserve everything we can give them, including connections of some sort with birth family. (It should also be noted that with the advent of Facebook, our children and their birth families may very well end up finding each other anyway.)

Like so much of adoption, open adoption is an emotional rather than an intellectual concept and decision, and it evokes strong emotions. Like so much of healthy adoptive family life at its best, the topic of open adoption needs wide ranging conversation, sharing of thoughts and feelings, and very likely the growth that so often happens!

Meeting our Son's Birth Father in Prison

Kristin Berry

Kristin lives in Indianapolis with her husband and six youngest children. She has two grown daughters, two sons in law, and a granddaughter as well. She spends her days juggling a part-time job as a Family Life Minister, blogging on *confessionsofanadoptiveparent.com,* and cleaning up after three dogs and four chickens. She enjoys reading, writing, and hiking with her family.

* * *

I am sitting in my car, hands pressed firmly to the steering wheel. My husband is staring out the passenger window at the correctional facility looming before us. The sky, grey with the threat of rain, only adds to this sense of anxious unknowing. The hour-long drive has brought nothing but silence from our three-year-old. His constant jabbering has been replaced with an uncommon quiet. We have not quite found a way to explain this visit to our pre-school son. He has always known we are not his biological parents. Caseworkers, supervised visits, and court hearings have been the norm for him since his arrival into the foster care system at three-days-old.

I glance at the clock and notice we have fifteen minutes left to wait. Our fate as a family rests on this moment. A court appointed visit to the prison. My husband and I make eye contact, and he squeezes my hand. I let go of the steering wheel, my hands aching from the intensity of my grasp. We both turn to our son and he smiles. That sweet, innocent grin I love so much. I make a goofy face at him and his smile widens. I know in the depths of my heart he is ours. He is also his, this man I know nothing about. Well, I know a little. A quick Google search of my son's birth father, left me with more information than I had ever wanted to know. After I finished reading pages of police reports, I carefully closed my laptop and tip-toed into my son's bedroom. I placed my hand over his heart and thanked God for his birth parents and the road that brought this little one to safety during an uncertain time in his life. That night I asked God to show me more about this father than what I read in the reports. So here I am about to get the chance to see him, face to face. I am about to look him in the eye and see if he is more than a criminal.

"Are you ready?" my husband asks. Surprisingly, I am. My heart is at peace. We take our son out of his car seat and walk to the back of the car. We remove our treasures. Wedding bands, jewelry, watches, earrings, the cute little toe ring I have had for 12 years takes a little bit of work to get off, and I chuckle at the absurdity of it. My laugh sounds far away. After securing our valuables in the trunk, we kneel down next to our child and squeeze his little hands. "We are going to meet your birth dad today. We will have to talk to a lot of people and go through a lot of doors. You may have to stand very still while someone checks your pockets but don't worry. Mommy and Daddy will be right next to you. Ok?" We use our very best calm voices. "Ok, I'm not scared," he answers back with the confidence only a pre-schooler can muster. We walk through the parking lot hand in hand just the three of us, filled with masked uncertainty.

The guards are unfriendly when we arrive, and they are not amused by our little one. He smiles at each of them anyway in his carefree way, and finally I think he wins one of them over. I catch the younger guard give my son a quick wink before returning to the task of patting me down and checking the bottoms of my feet. "What could I possibly have smuggled on the bottom of my feet?" I wonder. I don't dare ask. I am approved to go through the metal detector, so I follow my husband. This leaves my son on the other side to complete his customary pat down. He tears up and whimpers, "Mommy, don't leave me here." I whisper my encouragement back to him. "Don't worry, Daddy and I are right here." I am starting to get annoyed with how the guards are treating him. Can't they see he's afraid? My husband assures him, "You're doing a great job son. You're almost done." The older guard finishes checking his pockets, hands, and feet and directs him through the metal detector. He freezes. I go back to get him but the guards will not let me pick him up. We reach out our hands for him and he runs through the metal detector into our arms. I glare at the guard, my patience running thin. My son has done nothing wrong and neither have we. We have been court ordered to be here, and we are trying to be cooperative. My initial sense of peace is running out.

We follow the younger guard to another set of doors, and I am thankful that the older one is staying behind. He unlocks a giant door and motions for us to follow him. As we enter, I realize that we are in a very tiny room with doors on either end. The guard locks the door behind us then calls for permission to unlock the 2nd door. For a minute we are completely locked inside, and I feel my heart begin to pound. I am hopeful that my son does not sense my unease. I think he does though or is experiencing some of his own. He squeezes my hand, and I squeeze his and smile. My husband grabs his other hand. The guard unlocks the second door, and we follow him to another locked door. We enter into a larger room filled with small tables and stools. We are directed to sit at one of the tables. The guard warns that there is to be no touching, no hugging, and that we are to stay seated the entire time. Upon further inspection, we realize that the chairs and tables are bolted to the floor. We all take a seat and our three year old sits quietly like a little gentleman.

We watch as other visitors are ushered into the room to wait. After a while, the inmates enter the opposite end of the room in a single file line. They wait, hands at their sides, in the front of the room. As they are being dismissed to specific tables, I look over each of their faces. I scan the group and my eyes settle on someone familiar. Immediately I know this is my son's biological father. He is shorter, like my son. He spots us and smiles. There is something about that smile. I would know it anywhere. It is the same smile I look at every day. My heart softens a little. We are the same age, I remember.

He was just a kid once. When did childhood leave him and this become his circumstance? I will probably never know the answer, but the thought leaves me with a new perspective. He is not just a criminal; he isn't even just my son's birth dad. He is a human.

The visit flies by, and I am proud of my son for staying engaged in the conversation between the adults the whole time. We find common ground and talking is pretty easy. Birth dad is respectful toward us, and I am grateful that he is not pushy with our son. He asks good questions about the child and about us. He is especially interested in knowing how our son fits in with our family. He wants to know about all the brothers, sisters, and pets. He is interested to find that we had to give a cat away because of our son's serious allergy to cats. He is allergic too.

Finally, he opens the subject we have come here to discuss. I am thankful it is he who brings it up. "I appreciate you guys coming here. I know this is hard. I will sign the papers. It is not fair to leave him waiting in the system until I get out of here." My husband responds, and I am so thankful. Tears are welling up in my eyes, and I am afraid my voice will crack if I speak just now. My husband nods his head, "Thank you. You have no idea what this means to us. We love him so much. We want you to know, we will always be respectful and kind when we talk to our son about you. We will never put you down or make him feel ashamed of you. Thank you for meeting with us as well." All three of us look at our little son and he looks back at us carefully examining our faces, then he smiles at all three of us. The three of us know that this relationship is not about any of us, it is about the security and identity of this little person whom we all love. In this moment we are a family. An unconventional one, but a family nonetheless.

As the visitation comes to a close we cover the details of future visits. We will not visit again in the prison. We all agree that this is not the place for our son. We take some time to look over the recommendations made for future visitation by the guardian ad litem. We agree to the terms and if we were allowed to touch we would shake hands. The guard calls the inmates back, and we nod at one another one last time. An agreement has been made, and I feel the hopefulness of our new future before us.

The Other Mother

Kristin Berry

Kristin lives in Indianapolis with her husband and six youngest children. She has two grown daughters, two sons in law, and a granddaughter as well. She spends her days juggling a part time job as a Family Life Minister, blogging on *confessionsofanadoptiveparent.com* and cleaning up after three dogs and four chickens. She enjoys reading, writing, and hiking with her family.

* * *

Foster and adoptive parenting brings with it a unique relationship between two sets of parents. My husband and I are adoptive parents of eight children. Seven of our children have open adoptions. We have been fortunate to have good relationships with the birth parents of our children. As much as it depends on us, we strive to keep those relationships healthy and strong. We do this for our own sake, but more importantly for our children. Sometimes those bonds are as tricky as they are vital.

This is a story about one of those relationships. It all began when my son came to live with us at the age of ten-months. He had suffered neglect and witnessed horrific violence in his first home. He experienced homelessness and malnutrition. He was exposed to drugs and alcohol before birth and was born pre-maturely. My son did not sleep through the night for two years. We first noticed that he was not developing at a typical rate when he was about 16 months old. His happy mood would change to anger without cause. No one could identify the trigger. His anger was not the typical 'terrible twos' and tantrums lasted for up to eight hours. We were at a loss as to how to help him cope. So much of his trauma happened during his first year of life. His birth mother did not feed him, did not hold him, and did not protect him. By the time he came to live in our home, he was underweight, underdeveloped, scared, and untrusting. His birth mother should be the last person on earth that I would want to have a relationship with, but she isn't. Over the last twelve years I have come to know her as a person who was damaged by generations of abuse. She was perpetuating the cycle of abuse and neglect that had been a part of her family since before her birth. The day I realized that our lives could have been reversed was the day I saw her as the hurting child she had once been. I saw that I was a product of my environment as she had been a product of her own. When I realized I could easily have been in her shoes, I changed my attitude from anger to understanding.

Twelve years into our relationship, we had a conversation that took our relationship from polarization to unity. I had just met my son's birth mom for lunch, and as I drove home, I took some time to reflect. I pressed lightly on the brake as I listened to the "click click" of the turn signal. I gulped a breath of heavy air and relished in the uniqueness of this silence. It was that special kind of quiet, recently full of spoken words. As I turned onto the empty street the conversation tumbled about in my mind. I glanced back at the apartment complex to see my son's birth mom give a final wave. As I watched the city fade in my rearview mirror, I thanked God silently not just for my son but also for his 'Other Mother.'

We had just completed a lengthy discussion about the state of affairs with our shared child. On paper, it would seem that I am the mom that should have all the answers. I am the one who took over the parenting responsibility when she no longer could. I have always had the upper hand, more money, more education, a stable upbringing, and freedom from addiction. On paper we seem to have nothing in common. But, in reality, we share the thing that matters the most, our son.

So many of our conversations consist of me encouraging her as she makes her way in life, struggles with guilt and tries to make a better future for herself. This time she was my encourager, my strength, and my voice of reason and wisdom.

This conversation was one of our most difficult. I had to tell her that our son is currently in residential treatment. I had been holding back for weeks because I just did not want to admit that his mental illness was completely out of control. I did not want to admit how ill equipped I was to deal with his extreme behaviors. Mostly, I did not want her to feel I had not held up my end of the bargain when I adopted him.

I promised to care for him. I was afraid that she might think his behavior was my fault. I was also afraid she would think I was blaming her. My fear was nearly paralyzing as I haltingly shared the details of what brought our family to this point. I finished by saying, "I miss him." My voice trailed off as my eyes welled with the tears I desperately did not want her to see. Her response stunned me.

"I know you feel sad, and I know you miss him, but you have to let him get to the bottom before he'll ever want to climb out of this hole. He's making this choice, not you. You have to let him suffer this consequence even though it hurts you to see him hurting."

She then proceeded to tell me her story. We talked for over an hour about the road she walked before we met. She told me of thirteen foster and group homes. She told me of abandonment, fear, and shame. She told me of misplaced rage and the failed relationships that followed including the one with our son. She let me take a peek into her soul.

She never made an excuse for her choices. She shared the hurt others had done to her but never allowed the conversation to stay there. She admitted the hurt that she had done. She described the dark cavern of life she had been hurled into as a child and described how her choices had dropped her deeper and farther away from hope.

She ended by telling me that there was a moment, when life was at its darkest that she knew she was at the bottom of that hole. She knew that she was repeating the cycle of abuse, anger and abandonment that she learned growing up. In that moment, she picked herself up, looked at the tiny glimmer of hope that was left in her life and said, "ENOUGH! It's time to cut this out. It's time to change!"

I was thankful for the story. I needed to hear someone else say that all is not lost with our son. There is hope for him and for his future. I am so thankful that I did not close our relationship when my son's adoption was finalized. I could have walked away from her in disgust and anger. Even when I wanted to abandon our relationship I couldn't. Every time I look at my son, I see her eyes. I see her smile in my son's grin. I hear his laugh mirrored in hers. I am glad I did not walk away from my son's first mom. My son and I are both so lucky to have the love of his Other Mother.

A Birth Mother's Perspective on Open Adoption

Annie Jacobs

Annie Jacobs is a Midwesterner at heart who has lived in New York City for the past eleven years. She is a theatre professional who has educated herself on the complexities of adoption after relinquishing her only child in 2010. Since her son was born, she has spent her time cultivating a relationship with her son and his adoptive parents—a gay couple who also live in the city. She spends some of her spare time trying to educate others about what open adoption can be and what her experience as a birth parent has been.

* * *

On a Thursday in May six-years-ago, my son was born. Like most, after the birth of a child, my world was turned upside-down. My heart was filled with love, more than I knew was possible, and he became the center of everything for me. I understood what people meant when they talked about having a child, how it was like having a chunk of your heart existing outside of your body. I knew a new kind of all-encompassing love that day, the day I became a Mother.

The following Saturday, I signed TPR (termination of parental rights) paperwork and legally relinquished the right to parent my child. Magically everything was different, and I had this qualifier put in front of my title as Mother. The qualifiers people use are varied – a biological mother, a natural mother, an original mother, a first mother, a birth mother, but to me, it never really mattered which qualifier someone used after that day, the fact that a qualifier is used means I am no longer seen as other mothers are. After that moment, I was no longer considered a parent by most people. The hard part is although my title and the way people view me changed that day, my feelings for my son never changed; the connection always continued to be there. He was (and is) still the center of my world; I just stopped being the center of his.

For those who have never experienced relinquishment themselves, it is hard to concisely explain what it feels like to become a mother with a qualifier, what it means to relinquish. My social worker at the time equated it to the loss of having a child die. That did not quite fit for me; there was the pain and loss of losing my son, but it was never as concrete or as simple as death. How can you grieve for a person who you can still see and talk to? How can you feel the loss of a child when you still have a relationship with them? When I try to explain to outsiders the response I get most often is "well at least you can still see him; you know how he is doing. At least you can see that he is okay; you have the best of both worlds." I think before I relinquished I believed that was what openness was about, helping alleviate the loss for the biological parents, giving them the ability to see their child was in a good place.

In fact, I told my social worker as much when she tried to broach the subject about openness for the first time. I was almost eight months pregnant and had gotten as far into the adoption process as choosing a family to place with—a gay couple who lived local to me (Marty and Patrick). They were interested in openness. My response was "that will just complicate this kid's life. I don't want to complicate things for him just to try to make things easier on me." My social worker made it clear that I was not the most important factor in the equation; that openness at its pure root is for the adoptee. I listened at that moment, I took it in. I am glad I did.

After my son was born, I began to really understand openness on a different level. Adoption complicates things. At its core - being parented by people who are not your biological parents is complicated. The point of openness is not to further complicate things, but rather give an adoptee tools from the beginning to start to make sense of their already complicated life. Once my son was born I realized how right she was, we were connected in a way I could not even imagine before. I began to realize my son had this biological connection which was not going away and very quickly he grew a connection to the family raising him; openness was giving him the tools to acknowledge all the different parts of his identity and the different ways he was connected to those around him.

Focusing on what I believed was best for my son gave me a reason to put effort into an open relationship with his family. I am glad that was my focus from the beginning because within minutes of our first visit, I realized this path was going to be a difficult one for me. I am sure every open adoption experience differs from others, but for me, from the beginning visits were hard. I loved being with my son, seeing him, enjoying him. But the issue I had was the little boy in front of me was not the same little boy I had known in the hospital. From our first visit at six weeks old, I realized the child who I held in the hospital was being replaced by this baby who was adopted by Marty and Patrick. During my time in the hospital, my son – who I had named Jacob – was so clearly connected to me. It felt so right to hold him, I could recognize his cry, and he even seemed to smell different from every other baby. I did not doubt I was Jacob's Mother for any of those moments. But the day I signed the papers and handed him over to his Dads, something changed. It was not that his name was changed to Grayson Jacob, something I understood would happen even before he was born; the real change was he became more than the baby who I knew so well, he became someone who had connections beyond me. At our first visit, I was uncomfortable holding him mostly because he did not fit in my arms the same way he had before. I had to confront how this was not the same child I left at the hospital – his Dads knew his cries, knew what he needed, they were the ones who he looked to for comfort.

As the years went on we continued to have visits, at first every three months or so, then as time went on they became more frequent. By his third year I saw him on average once a month. The feelings of loss I felt changed with each visit, each contact I had with my son and his family. The feelings did not necessarily go away, but they did begin to evolve, and I learned to navigate through them. I accepted that loss and grief would always be a part of my relationship, and that allowed me to focus on my son and grow our relationship.

It can be difficult to talk about the feelings of loss in the adoption community when you are a part of a healthy open adoption. People seem to think I should feel gratitude because seemingly against the odds I have a very strong relationship with my son. To talk about the loss does not mean I cannot simultaneously feel gratitude about the amazing little boy and my ongoing relationship with him. There is such a joy in having this relationship, not just because I see my son, but because I have been welcomed into his extended family. I am incredibly grateful these people who love my son have brought me into their lives, but I do feel it is necessary to acknowledge there is another side to this, that even in a healthy open adoption there is still loss because otherwise I think it is too easy assume openness is a remedy to all problems of adoption, especially the grief of the biological parents.

As Grayson grew and our relationship evolved, Grayson's own awareness and feelings became another part of this relationship that we needed to focus on. By age two he had started asking real questions – although he knew me as Annie, he was not really certain how I fit into his world. By three, he was certain; he began to be able to talk about his family using the language he was comfortable with, and I became a part of that narrative. Adoptees often talk about issues they face in identity and family. I can see my son at the young age of six starting to discover how he fits in this world and how he fits into his family. Sometimes those discoveries can be difficult to process, but because of openness he has tools at his fingertips to start to understand his story and define his family. Both his biological family and his adoptive family are at his side helping him traverse this tricky ground.

This is not the way all open adoptions look. I do not know exactly why ours has turned out this way. I have heard people say it is because Grayson has two Dads thus I am not competing with them; others have said it is because we are from similar backgrounds and social classes so the adults are comfortable with each other; some think it is in part because we were local to each other. I don't think there is any one thing to point to; all these have played a factor. But I think for us the most important factor was that all of us decided this relationship was more important than our own insecurities and doubts. Again and again Marty and Patrick have acknowledged my connection to Grayson, whether it is by telling someone his eye color comes from me, or using their knowledge that I loved the water from an early age and putting Grayson into swim classes. They celebrate the ways Grayson is like me, and this attitude has been a gift for me. Having spoken to other adoptive parents, I know it can be hard to celebrate a connection your child has to someone else, especially because it is not a connection you share yourself. Similarly it can be difficult for me to see my son's connection to his parents, to know if he falls down, he is going to need his Dads to make it feel better, and that if he learns a new fact they are the first ones he wants to tell. Those moments which make it so clear I am not the one parenting him can make me feel insecure about my role in his life. I have chosen to let go of those insecurities and instead celebrate the ways Grayson is a part of this amazing family who loves him so completely. It is not always easy to do – to acknowledge that another person is connected with your child in a way you never will be, but it has been important that we do this for this relationship to be successful.

The success of our relationship also required all of us to navigate what are sometimes unclear boundaries in our relationship. From my perspective that meant acknowledging that Marty and Patrick were the overseers of this relationship; they had the control over how much access I had to Grayson. I worried for a long time about making a wrong move and pushing for too much; I knew that stepping over a boundary could have consequences. I was told by so many that most open adoptions close, and for a long time I waited for that to be the fate of ours. I wanted to do everything in my power to make ours flourish, and it seemed the key was to respect boundaries, but I often had no idea where those boundaries were. What made this so difficult was the lack of examples of other relationships like ours. In society, most of our decisions about relationships are based on our insights gleaned from observing others. You cannot go a day without observing all kinds of different relationships – mother and child, husband and wife, boyfriends, girlfriends, friends, teacher and student, boss and employee - and you use those observations to set the course of your own relationships, sometimes by emulating them and other times by using them as cautionary tales. That sort of observation did not exist for me; until I was living one I had no idea what an open adoption could or should look like. This total lack of examples made the questions on boundaries very difficult for me. I stumbled through while constantly worrying that I was about to totally mess everything up.

So I spent the first few years trying to find the perfect balance between two extremes – my son knowing I am available to him in any capacity he needed and his Fathers understanding that I recognized they were the parents. I knew my son needed access to me and I wanted him to be able to look to me for information, but I also strongly felt I needed to do that without undermining my son's parents. I knew they were the adults making the decisions in my son's life, and I never wanted them to think I thought I knew better or that I did not have complete respect for them as parents. All this was difficult to navigate, but to put more pressure on the situation, the risk if I messed up was a relationship with my son, a relationship that I believe has great benefits to my son. I needed it to work for my benefit and for Grayson's, yet I had little confidence that I knew exactly how to do that.

But with the help of Marty and Patrick, I was able to keep going and figure out boundaries that worked for all of us. The difficult ground of the first few years of this relationship became a really strong foundation that we have built our relationship on. I no longer think about *if* they write back to an email I send, but *when* they will write back. And those times I don't hear back right away, my brain does not go to the dark place of what it means, but rather assumes they must be busy. I know they love me and that more importantly my son needs me in his life, from there I believe we will figure everything else out.

The thing I do want to be clear about is Marty and Patrick never said anything to make me think they were contemplating closing our relationship, none of their actions ever insinuated that I was not an appreciated part of their family. From the beginning they continually did things to seemingly make it easier on me – they quickly started the habit of talking about the next visit before leaving the last. They made sure I had time and opportunity to spend time with Grayson around his birthday and around Christmas. They invited me to both large family events (so I got to know Grayson's extended family) and planned visits that were just us so I could spend real and quality time with Grayson. And still with all they did for me, I worried all the time.

I worried that I could make a wrong move and everything would change. It was not until a few years in when Grayson and I started to really develop our own relationship that I finally felt secure that this all would not just dissolve. He was not even three when he started to ask really difficult questions, questions about why I did not live with him and his Daddies, or why I had to go back to my apartment at the end of a visit. These questions were difficult for me; there was not always a simple answer, and it was hard to watch my son struggle to try to understand. Marty and Patrick could have used it as an excuse – that this whole thing was too hard on Grayson; they didn't. Instead they acknowledged that adoption is difficult, and we would all openly talk about it and work through it, as a family.

I understood then that they were in this with me. I also really began to understand that I was needed. The truth is my son will continue to face hard realities in his life regarding adoption. He will know what it means to be nurtured by people who are not connected to him biologically. He will grow to understand that his whole family will never live under the same roof. He has to deal with the fact he may never meet some people related to him biologically. My son has to deal with a lot, he has to confront feelings as a toddler that I see adoptees entering reunion AS ADULTS struggle with – feelings of abandonment, feeling a deep love and loss simultaneously (a feeling I often struggle with), or the difficulty of not understanding why things are the way they are. But I have come to believe that those feelings may exist for him no matter if he is in an open adoption or not, and it is our job (his parent's and mine) to give him the language and the tools to talk about and deal with the emotions he feels.

Once I felt that, once I knew that, it only reiterated to me that **this was not about me**. My feelings were difficult, but I was the adult here. I was the one who made the decision to put adoption into my son's life. He did not have a choice. The least I could do for him was to not let my own fears and insecurities, loss and grief overtake my relationship with him. It does not make the day to day of our relationship any different, but knowing there is a purpose, a reason for traversing this bumpy ground, it helps me keep moving forward.

A few months after my son's fourth birthday, Marty and Patrick informed me of a decision they had made. They had decided to move their family to Hong Kong. Their decision was hard for me, knowing my son would be so far away. He was not old enough to write letters or emails, I am not a huge fan of FaceTime, and he would be 12 time zones away. But before I had any chance to freak out, they wanted to make sure I understood a few things. The most important thing was that I was a factor; my relationship with Grayson was a factor in their decision. I believe now that they would not have moved if they thought we would not be able to have a healthy long distance relationship. The move was precipitated by a job change, and they negotiated into the contract with the company that the company would fly me out once a year for a visit. This is a concession the company gives for immediate family members. For Marty and Patrick, I was part of Grayson's immediate family – I qualified.

They moved just over a year ago, and it has greatly changed things between us, but most surprisingly is how much has not changed. At its core, this all is about a relationship with my son. I still have that. Over Christmas I was playing cards with him. I grew up in a family that has always loved playing cards, so I learned to shuffle quite young. When I shuffle I do a bridge, and when he saw that he said "I like that bridge you're doing. Do you like the bridge too?" When I told him I did his reply was "Liking the same things is something we have in common. We have lots in common because you're my Mommy. I also have lots in common with my Daddies. Isn't that right?" Yes, Grayson, yes. For him, at that moment, adoption could be that simple. He is a little boy with two Dads and a Mom who lives on a different continent. He is a part of me, and he is a part of them. He is this mash up of all the good from all these different people who love him, some connected by nature, some connected by nurture. He has found a way to own all those parts of his identity and celebrate the relationships that go along with that.

I do not know if my son will grow up and continue to see his adoption so simply. It is hard to tell, there is not a lot of research about how adoptees who grow up in true open adoptions feel as adults. Even if there was research, I think I have to wait until Grayson's grown to see how *he* feels growing up in his particular version of family. Honestly, I do not know now if what we are doing is helping alleviate any of the issues adoptees can have or just shuffling what those issues are and how they manifest. But we are a family and so whatever feelings my son experiences, we are confronting them together. And today, that has to be enough.

Both And: Connections in Open Adoption

Joshua Redfern, LCSW

Josh likes to say that he "eats, sleeps, and breathes adoption." Before he graduated with a Masters in Social Work in 2007, Josh found his passion for adoption while doing an internship for an adoption agency. At the same time, he and his wife were being led to adoption personally. He has since worked in domestic adoption (both in agency and in independent adoptions) and international adoption. He has provided domestic and international home studies for families all over the world. He is an active member of the Utah Adoption Council and is an advocate for ethical adoption and open adoption. He has a wonderful wife, Lindsey, who is an adoption advocate and writer. They have been blessed to adopt five children.

* * *

My Path to Open Adoption

After a few years of marriage, my wife and I started actively trying to have children. We always wanted children and we were getting to a place in our lives where we felt comfortable starting a family. We made, what we see now as, ridiculously meticulous plans on just when and where our child would come into the world. We made adjustments as those timelines passed, only having to adjust again and again. Finally, we decided we needed to see what was going on. Pretty soon after, it became very clear that we would have a very hard time having children biologically. Due to some experiences I had professionally, we were able to learn more about adoption and feel comfortable with it as a way of starting a family.

I remember when I first heard of "open adoption." We had just started looking into adoption and we went to a panel of adoptive parents at our adoption agency. At least a couple of the families discussing their stories had very open relationships with their children's birth parents, something I had never thought of as a possibility. It was, honestly, a little scary. When you grow up thinking about how your family life will look, you just don't think about including this dynamic. What really started changing my heart is when we were able to witness a panel of birth moms. It was then that I realized a few things about birth parents.

First, birth parents are normal people. I don't think I ever had any real negative ideas about birth parents, but actually meeting some reinforced that they are people just like you and me. At first, actually, you start to sort of view them as perfect. You see their sacrifices, and you can really just be in awe of them. I have learned, since, that viewing birth parents like unicorns takes away from who they really are. They are human, with "good" and "bad" characteristics. Recognizing them as people that are just people has helped me to feel more comfortable having a relationship with them.

Second, birth parents LOVE their children. I have yet to come across a birth parent that does not have a great love for their child. I suppose there are some out there, but particularly when the adoption was voluntary, it is very rare. As I contemplated why I would or would not want an open adoption with my children's birth parents, the love that they have for them was a major factor in taking steps towards openness. If love motivates ME to do what is best for my child, wouldn't it also, in most cases, lead my children's birth parents to do what is best for the child, as well? Why would I want to prevent my child from that love? I was going to let SO many more people into my child's life that would, hopefully, love them (my parents, siblings, cousins, friends, etc), why not allow those that have at least as much (and maybe more) of a reason to love them than even I do?

Third, the birth parents in this panel did not want to co-parent and I have not found many since then, either, where that is the desire. I began to see that open adoption is not like being divorced. These birth parents were not asking to help dictate parenting decisions. They were actually very pleased to NOT have to be involved in some of those decisions or parental responsibilities. I began to realize, that in a healthy open adoption, I would not be competing with another parent. As time has borne out, this has definitely been true. In fact, our children have used the classic "My birth mom would let me do that!" and it has been nice to have their birth parents actually BACK UP our parenting.

As the years have gone by since that first introduction to open adoption, my attitude has completely changed. I actually would love MORE openness in most cases. We have varying degrees of contact with different biological relatives. Some are far physically but still close emotionally. Some are closer physically but the contact is not as frequent (per their desires). Some grandparents are more involved than others. Some appear to have a harder time with openness and some still do not seem to know what they want or need (they may even feel they do not know how to approach us about it). I have gotten to the point, though, where I wished they all lived close and we could communicate regularly. Sure, we would still keep healthy boundaries (as you would with any relationship) but I miss them because I love them. They are who my children come from. I love my children, so I love them. Technology has helped, though; texting, phone calls, emails, video chat, social media, etc. have all helped us stay in touch.

Open Adoption is About Making Connections We All Crave

"I love tomatoes" my son says while he eats a Roma tomato like someone else would eat an apple. This is something I have never seen anyone do, but here is my oldest son chomping one down like it is the most normal thing in the world.

"You know who also loves tomatoes—your birth mom!"

This is a variation of an interaction that happens in homes everywhere. We, as humans, crave connections. We want to know who is like us. We crave it so much that we volunteer this kind of information to those we care about because we "know" they need that connection too. If we can offer a connection to someone, we do it. Parents do this all of the time. We are just engrained with this idea. I do not think it is just some cultural quirk that has no meaning, either. It is more than that. It happens too often to just be some meaningless act. We do it when we look at old photos. We laugh at mom's terrible clothes and hair and then comment on how much alike you and her look at the same ages. It is just trickier when a child is adopted.

It took us a while to get it right. My wife and I grew up in fully biological families, so we learned how to do this the traditional way. "X characteristic/behavior is just like Y biological relative." Hearing that and then participating in it for twenty-plus-years gets engrained in you. Early in our parenthood of our five children that we have through adoption, we would catch ourselves doing this. We would say "You get your eyes from grandma." then kind of look at each other like "Yeaaaaaah, no he doesn't."

Sure, you can make connections despite biology. Grandma's and granddaughter's eyes may actually really look alike. It is okay to say that. But the do not come from them. Your child may pick up or have similar behaviors as your spouse. Make that connection; it probably IS a real connection. But that is not always what we are seeking. We are looking for a biological connection, for whatever reason, and we seem to want them in abundance, while abundance can be (or seem to be) lacking for an adoptee.

But, in Open Adoption, you can make these connections. If you know what your children's first/birth families look like, act like, sound like, you can help them make these connections. You can tell them where they get their nose from. You can tell them how their beautiful skin color is just like their beautiful biological mother's skin color. You can express to them that their incredible grasp of math is DEFINITELY not something that comes from you and is most certainly something that came from their biological grandpa. This NEED that we have to make connections can be made in their adoptive family AND their biological family. Both of those bonds can be strengthened.

I think one of the concepts that you need to work through, as an adoptive parent, to be able to support your child in making these connections is to deal with the idea of your child being "yours." During the finalization of our daughter's adoption, I started to think about the concept of a child being "mine." When we think about possession, we usually think in fairly linear/simplistic/concrete terms. You buy a television and it's "yours", you sell it and it's "theirs." Pretty straightforward. On paper, this is sort of what the legal process of adoption is. In terms of responsibilities and certain rights, the child is transferred from one parent (or set of parents) to another. But are children really

possessions like a television? Of course not! But we talk
like it sometimes.

Does me (or the judge) saying that my daughter is "mine"
take away from her being her biological mother's? Sure,
it does in some ways. I am now responsible for her in all
of those concrete ways that make you a parent (feeding,
clothing, making sure she does her homework, lecturing
her) that her biological parents are not. She is also "mine"
in that more spiritual, emotional attachment way. But is
she really no longer her biological mothers's daughter or
her biological grandparent's granddaughter?

In my opinion, no amount of paperwork takes away the
real connections between an adoptee and their biological
family. How can you really sever that relationship? These
two (and her other biological family) are inextricably tied
together, and not necessarily by blood or DNA as many
would say. The very act of a birth parent releasing their
legal rights to their child because of their love for that
child is one of the things that connects them forever. How
can an act so selfless really divide them?

I do not have a problem calling my children "mine" and
making connections with them. I also do not mind it if
their biological family calls them "theirs" and point out
that they look just like them. That does not take away
from the children being connected to me, it just means
they have other connections, too. We WANT our kids to
make other connections throughout their lives but we are
often afraid of them making those connections to those
people that REALLY are connected to them. We want
them to have friends, we want them to fall in love, we
want them to feel connected to their own children. But

we sometimes get scared or uncomfortable with pointing out how much they look like their biological family.

So, how do you help your children make these connections? Well, you have to get to really know their biological family. Many adoptions are technically "open" but there is still a lot of distance in the relationship. One of the things I have seen in a lot of adoptions is that you really do need to take advantage of the time you have before placement to gather a lot of this information. Perhaps you will not have the kind of open adoption that will allow for a lot of interaction later on, but you are often spending a lot of time getting to know each other prior to the birth. Take advantage of that. Ask TONS of questions. It does not have to be awkward, either. You can make it fun. Send get-to-know you questionnaires to each other. Ask to see pictures of them as kids. Ask who THEY look like or where they get their personality from. Ask for family stories. And WRITE IT ALL DOWN.

The benefit of a very open adoption is that you have a consistent source of information. With an open adoption where you regularly communicate, you just have a ton more time to gather data that can be used to help your children make connections. You can really know what their biological family is like. You have more opportunities to see what is similar between them and your child. Just the other day, my son called his birth mother to talk about allergies. They both have them, and they both HATE them! You get to hear more stories, meet more family members, see more old pictures. Recently, I have even been able to talk to our kids' biological families about their genealogy. There are hundreds of years of connections to make there. Incredible stories of flight from the Nazis, lines with Scottish royalty, and people trekking across country to find freedom.

Even better than the chance we have to help our children feel connected, in open adoption, our children can see those connections for themselves. We always accept things more when we see them ourselves. They can see where they get their curly hair and may even get good advice on how to handle it. It is one thing to have a child be told these things and another to be able to see it. Again, this is something that happens very often when a child is raised in their biological family. They are not just told about connections, they witness them on their own.

It is really important to seek after all the information you can about biological families. Unfortunately, in many adoptions, you may have received most of your information from one source. In many situations, you are hearing from the biological mother's side about the biological father's side. And, often, that relationship is not very good. I have heard adoptees who were told only bad things about one or both of their biological parents talk about the opposite of what I am talking about. When a person is told over and over again about how terrible their biological father is, they often start to feel like "If that's where I come from, then I must be bad, too." We do not often seek negative connections; we seek positive ones. We laud our kids with how great this one feature is and how it connects to someone else in the family. We want to believe we come from something good, so that we can feel we are capable of being good ourselves. If all we know (or care to know), as adoptive parents, are the bad things about our children's biology, then that is all our children will know. But none of them come from people that are pure evil. Everyone has wonderful things about them. It is important to learn what those things are and make those connections.

You may also have had some struggles in open adoption. Whether it was boundaries being crossed, hard feelings from certain members of the biological family or miscommunications, it is important to try to repair these relationships. Again, what does this say to your children if we do not want to have good relationships with where they come from? Sure, sometimes things get unsafe, but there can always be some repair assuming that you are not harboring hard feelings even if you do not communicate them. We have had some great experiences reaching out to biological family that were not supportive of adoption previously and there were really hard feelings. Unkind things were said and thought on both sides. But, because I was able to see that my child needed a connection to their biological family, I had to get over my own personal hurt. Like the title of this book, **it's not about ME. It's about the needs of my child.**

Research tells us that Open Adoption can be beneficial to everyone, especially the adoptee. In research done with adolescents, the majority were satisfied that they had continuing contact. Other demonstrated benefits were:

coming to terms with the reasons for their adoption

physical touchstones to identify where personal traits came from

information that aids in identity formation

positive feelings toward birthmother.

Adolescents involved in these kind of adoptions also have a better understanding of the meaning of adoption and more active communication about adoption with their adoptive parents (Berge, et al., 2006; Grotevant, et al., 2007; Wrobel, et al., 1996 & 1998).

When we are going through an adoption "best interest of the child" is the phrase that we say drives the decisions, but we often let our own concerns about the "difference", "weirdness", or "fear" of open adoption to get in the way of what our kids really need. We can still be their parents. We do not have to be replaced, forgotten, pushed aside. But we also should not replace forget or push aside the very real connections that our children have with their biological families. Let them make those connections, helping them do so can strengthen your connection with them.

REFERENCES

Berge, J. M.; Mendenhall, T. J.; Wrobel, G. M.; Grotevant, H. D.; & McRoy, R. G. (2006). Adolescents' Feelings about Openness in Adoption: Implications for Adoption Agencies.*Child Welfare League of America, 85.6,* 1011-1039. doi: 0009-4021/2006/0501011-28. Retrieved from: http://search.proquest.com/openview/f18aa63d3ee46d9fe a0a86d2b0d46f72/1?pq-origsite=gscholar.

Grotevant, H. D.; Wrobel, G. M.; Von Korffc, L.; Skinner, B.; Newell, J.; Friesec, S.; & McRoy, R. G. (2007). Many Faces of Openness in Adoption:Perspectives of Adopted Adolescents and Their

Parents. *Adoption Quarterly, 10,* 79-101. doi: 0.1080/10926750802163204.

Wrobel, G. M.; Ayers-Lopez, S.; Grotevant, H. D.; McRoy, R. G.; & Friederick, M. (1996). Openness in Adoption and the Level of Child Participation. *Child Development, 67,* 2358-2374. doi: 10.2307/1131628.

Wrobel, G. M.; Kohler, J. K.; Grotevant, H. D.; & McRoy, R. G. (1998). Factors related to patterns of information exchange between adoptive parents and children in mediated adoptions. *Journal of Applied Developmental Psychology, 19,* 641-657. doi: 10.1016/S0193-3973(99)80060-4.

Committing to Open International Adoption

Mary McBride

Mary McBride is an American turned Londoner, a wife to a tech geek husband, a mother of two Ethiopian daughters, a home educator, and a chocolate and doughnut enthusiast. She is passionate about adoptive parent education, adoptee rights, open adoption, and pursuing best case scenarios for children who have experienced trauma. She might not get things right the first time, but she will keep trying.

* * *

When we set out to begin our international adoption, we knew that we wanted to keep our child connected to her culture. The days of social workers recommending assimilation into the family were over, and we knew it would be important to keep our daughter connected to her birth culture and to make a way for her to visit her birth country as part of the healthy formation of her identity. We were advised on ways to celebrate her heritage and to tell her the story of her origins, to answer her questions openly and to help her navigate her feelings as a transracial adoptee. However, no one in the trainings we attended ever mentioned the possibility of open adoption. We had a sense that we would want to be in contact with our daughter's relatives if there were any who desired that, but the idea of open international adoption was rather vague.

However, the more we spoke to adult adoptees and read what they were writing, the more we understood that if we could keep our child connected to her first family, which would be best for her. So we began to entertain the idea of establishing an open international adoption - not just sending reports back to our daughter's home country that her family could obtain from the orphanage to read, followed by participating in agency-arranged meetings, but being in regular contact personally. When our daughter came into our family at the age of three years, with memories of her early life, it became clearer to us that it was the right way to proceed.

We believe that it should be the adoptee's decision to whether or not to search and make connections, but since our daughter was so young, we recognized that we would need to make the decision on her behalf. We made this decision for her primarily, but also in light of what we knew of her family members and their desires. We wanted to honor both our daughter and her first family, as none of them had any control over the series of events which led to her need for an adoptive family. And so we began almost immediately after her adoption to lay the groundwork for an open international adoption.

The process of establishing the open adoption relationship is different for each family. In our experience, it has not been a linear process, and it has not been easy. But we are committed to it, and we intend to keep pressing forward to achieve the end result of a well-established relationship between our daughter and her first family, that she can continue in whatever way she chooses as she grows. This is the story of the first part of our process and what we hope will occur in the future. To us, the key has been our commitment. When things have not gone as planned, we remain committed to the goal.

In our daughter's birth country, it is fairly common for there to be misinformation on the adoption paperwork. Prior to her adoption, we did not understand how widespread this issue was; the prevailing wisdom at that time was that if you chose an ethical agency, everything would be above board and fine. Particularly if you met with a family member, which we did, it was considered to be highly likely that everything was correctly done in the process. It was when we brought our daughter home with us that we started to hear more and more stories of details changed or left out of the paperwork for adoptions done by supposedly ethical agencies. This gave us all the more reason to make contact with her family. We wanted the true story for our daughter, and more than the paperwork could tell us, but we also wanted to make sure that she truly needed to be adopted.

This was the source of my greatest fear during the process. Of course we were nervous about the usual things. Would her family members like us and think we were doing a good job? Would we be able to bridge language and cultural divides? Those are valid sources of nervousness, but nothing compared to my worry that she did not need us after all, that she had suffered all that hurt and loss for no reason. We knew that if that was the case, we would have to figure out how to move forward with resettling her with her first family. We loved her completely already, and we could not imagine life without her. As much as we knew what the right thing to do would be, we also knew that it would be very painful for us to do it.

Many agencies offer services to be in touch with family, but if they are operating from documents with incorrect information, then they will not be effective in helping with continued communication. If they have behaved unethically or turned a blind eye to unethical practices at the orphanage level, they will be most interested in protecting their own reputation. The best way to get true information and establish contact with the appropriate people is to send a searcher.

We heard about our first searcher through word of mouth; someone else had used his services and gotten a good result, and we felt his fees were appropriate for the work involved. When we hired him, we went in fairly blindly, knowing that we wanted correct information about our daughter's first family and a way to keep in continued contact, but not having defined the best way to do this. It is fair to say that we muddled our way through the process with the first searcher, and we learned a lot along the way.

Our first searcher located our daughter's family after a few false leads. (We had met a family member at the time the adoption was completed, so we had a little bit of information to go on beyond the error-riddle paperwork, and we were able to confirm that a person in one of the photos the searcher sent was the relative we had previously met.) We were provided with a good deal of information we did not have before, plus additional details that confirmed that the adoption was necessary. That was all very valuable to us. We also agreed to set up a post office box so we could send correspondence to the family, and that seemed like a good plan to us.

A year after this first contact through the searcher, we traveled to our daughter's birth country for a second adoption. We contacted the searcher to facilitate a meeting with some of our daughter's family members, and he made the necessary arrangements for us. It was during this meeting that we started to understand that we needed to make some adjustments to our methods of communication.

Because the child we were adopting was medically fragile, we asked family members to come to the capital to meet us. We provided funds for the family's transportation and for a guest house for them to stay in during the visit, then paid for all of their needs while they were in the capital. The searcher facilitated all of this, as well as arranging for translators, and we paid a fee to him for his services, which included the fees he paid to the translators. Additionally, we paid for the food everyone ate while they were with us, both the family and the searcher, plus translators.

We spent two days visiting with our daughter's family, and all meetings were in the hotel where we were staying for the adoption. Admittedly, this was not ideal, but it was what we could make work at that time, and we felt it was more important that our daughter and her family members see each other than it be the perfect meeting. The first time our daughter and her family saw each other, it was in the hotel lobby. Everyone was ecstatic, but trying to keep quiet since we were in public. There were several times that we felt things were awkward because we were in public, but there was not much we could do to change that on short notice, with a medically fragile baby to care for at the same time.

Because our daughter's family speaks a different dialect than the national language, we had two translators for the visit. This was our second point of awkwardness, and our first clue that it would be better to find someone else to help us. Whatever was said had to got through two translators. We did not get to say much because it took so long for each thing to be translated. At that time, I made a mental note that if possible, it would be best to find a translator who spoke English and our daughter's dialect. There were many children adopted from her region, and there is a nearby university, so I knew it would not be impossible to find someone who spoke the national language, her family's dialect, and English.

Overall, the first visit was a good one for many reasons. Our daughter had begun to lose some of her memories of her home country and her relatives, and it was healing for her to be able to see and speak with and hug her family members. They, too, were happy to be able to meet. They spoke of being relieved to see her healthy and growing well, and to be able to observe that we were treating her as a true daughter, that she was very well loved. While the visit was far from ideal, it helped set to rest a lot of worries that existed for all of us, and that in and of itself made it worth it.

However, during the visit, we began to see some red flags with our searcher. He invited extra people to the meals we were paying for. He asked us for additional money to fund his searching business. Then he revealed that he was a former employee of an adoption agency that we knew to be highly unethical. Before the visit ended, we attempted to get more specific information about the location of our daughters' relatives' home, and he would not give it to us. This, even more than the language issue, confirmed to us that we did not want to work with him any longer, that someone else could do a better job for us.

After we returned home to the United States and got settled, we began to research other searchers. We knew we would not be able to return to our daughter's birth country for a while, but we wanted to establish contact through a new source as soon as we were able. We could continue to send things to the post office box for the additional year that we had paid for it be held in our daughter's relatives' names, so we determined to do that as a stop gap measure until contact could be established.

After our negative experience with the first searcher, we resolved to do a better job choosing our next one. We contacted nearly everyone that we knew who had done a search in our daughter's region, and we got as many recommendations as possible. We chose a searcher based on recommendations and skills. Our new searcher was from our daughter's region and spoke her dialect, as well as the national language and English. Because he was from the region, he also knew the culture well and could guide us as we navigated cultural issues.

By the time we arranged for the services of this second searcher, it had been nearly two years since we saw our daughter's relatives in the capital, and nearly a year since we had sent our last correspondence to the post office box. This is the maximum time we set for ourselves to be in contact again, and we just barely met that goal. We sent the new searcher to check in with the family and deliver a message from us as soon as possible, as we felt this was far too long to go without contact. He was able to visit the family in their home village and give us far more detailed information than the other searcher did.

Shortly thereafter, we prepared for a visit to the village, and he facilitated that visit, as well as acting as translator and guide for us. The second visit took place over the course of two days, with the first day spent in our daughter's village, and the second in a nearby city. We hired a driver to take us from the capital to the region our daughter is from and drive us to and from the village, then drive us back to the capital at the end of the weekend. We were able to see where our daughter was born and spent her early years, plus meet everyone who had a part in her adoption so we could hear the full story of how she came to be part of our family in addition to being part of theirs. We spent an extended time period simply asking questions of one another and finding out more about each other.

There was far less discomfort on this second visit. It was much more comfortable for the family to be in their own home environment, and our daughter was thrilled to see her old home again and to explore the village. Family members from all over the region showed up to greet her, and most people from the village joined in the festivities. There was very little privacy afforded to us or to her first family, so for the second day, we arranged to meet for a quiet meal in a hotel in the nearest city. We had gifts for the family which we did not want to flaunt in front of the entire village, so this was an appropriate place to present those gifts. Our daughter had chosen many of the gifts, and it was a special time for her to be able to present them to the people she loves.

At the end of the visit, we set out our hopes for continued contact. The family told us that the post office box did not work well for them, so we agreed to visit when we can and to send the searcher with messages in between visits. The searcher can receive photos by email and print them in country for delivery to her family with the message we send. This is not optimal, but it is where we are starting, now that we have a searcher we trust who can also act as translator for messages.

In many ways, it feels like we are just getting started with regular contact, even though our daughter has been part of our family for five years now. There were challenges we did not expect, and we are not as far along the road of open international adoption as I had hoped we would be. But now we know that we should expect challenges, and we know what challenges exist that we need to address.

The first challenge was that our first searcher proved to be untrustworthy. Had things gone smoothly with him, we likely would have better contact at this point. There was no way to know when we hired him that this was the case. Searching was still a fairly new thing for adoptive families in our daughter's country at that point, so our mistakes became part of the lesson from which others can learn. We now recommend that families do extensive research into their searchers and only hire someone who is well recommended by all families who have used his or her services.

Our second challenge was (and is) the dual challenge of language and cultural barriers. Our culture is quite different from our daughter's birth culture, and there is a lot of room for missteps. We will need a trusted guide for the long term, in addition to simply needing a translator. Our searcher is very good about helping us to understand culture, but we have had to accept that there will be awkward moments along the way.

The third challenge is financial issues. We did not do our first search as soon as we hoped because we had to save to have enough to afford it. Of all the things we did not know when we went into the international adoption process, I think the one we underestimated the most was how much it would cost to procure the services we would need to keep in contact and make regular visits. We would like to be in touch more frequently than we are, but we cannot currently afford to send the searcher multiple times per year for the fee he charges for the family visit. Similarly, we would like to visit more often, but a trip is expensive, and we cannot afford it as often as we had hoped we would be able to.

The fourth challenge is complacency. It is shockingly easy to forget how long it's been since our last communication, and in our comfortable life, it is far too easy to just let things go for weeks or months longer than we should. Life moves fast when kids are involved, and we are sometimes guilty of placing more importance on day to day life than making sure we are communicating on our proposed schedule. I know it is important for my daughter and for her family that we are in touch, but sometimes the importance I should place on that slips.

he fifth challenge is simply managing our expectations, particularly in terms of timeline. At this point, we had hoped to be visiting family annually and sending a report at the six month mark between visits. But we are still on a biennial visiting schedule, which may stretch longer since we have a second child and thus a second family to visit. I feel discouraged that we have not done a better job of meeting our goals and that can lead to feeling like nothing we do is good enough.

Knowing all that, it is still our intention to continue to proceed so that we can meet the goals we have set as soon as it is possible for us. The first thing we are doing is addressing the frequency of communication and visits. We are communicating with our daughter's first family to find out what will work best for them and what they are willing to do in order to see her and hear from her. We know that they are willing to have us visit them at any time in their village, and we are seeking to find out their openness to meeting with us in a nearby city as well as in the capital. We know that travel to the capital is very stressful for them, but we have not yet established if they would feel it is worth it to visit us there if we cannot go to their village.

We are also seeking alternate means of communication. While we feel it is best to send a message annually with the searcher so it can be translated appropriately, we need to find out if anyone they know has a cell phone and can pass messages on to them, or if anyone has internet access and could connect with us on Facebook so we can send photos more frequently. We would also like to give them a way to send messages to us instead of having to wait on our communications schedule. The relationship will not truly be open if we control all the means of communication.

We now proceed with the intention of establishing consistent communication and visits. We are in touch with our searcher annually to send photos and a report of the past year. We have chosen a month during which communication from us will always occur, whether that is sending word with the searcher or going ourselves for a visit. We aim to make this predictable both for our daughter and for her first family, but also to be flexible if a different time of year is better for a visit.

As our daughter grows older, we want to be sensitive to her wishes for how contact is conducted. As the only person in the scenario who did not have a choice about the adoption itself, it is most important to listen to her hopes, wishes, and intentions for contact with her first family. As much as we are able, we hope to accommodate her desires. Over time, we hope to establish a way for her to connect with her family without our help. We will always help if she wants us to, but we want her to have ownership of the relationship. This is her story, and her family. We are laying the foundation, but what she builds is up to her.

If you are considering establishing contact for an open international adoption, I would encourage you to do it as soon as you are able. The longer you wait, the harder it may become to find the information you need to make and maintain contact. Details of your child's story which were fresh in the minds of family, friends, and neighbors may grow hazy.

As you commit to the process, do your best to set aside any expectations for how the process will go. It is different for everyone, and it is a relationship. The important part is that you are committed to it. Be patient with your searcher. Be mindful of how you are feeling about the search and if you could use additional support from a therapist or from a group of people who are pursuing the same thing. If your child is old enough to be part of the process, be mindful of his or her needs for support, both from you and from a therapist or support group or mentor.

Finally, I encourage you to go forward with courage. It can be scary to navigate this. It can take a lot of time and effort and frustration and discomfort, but it is worth it. This will provide your child with knowledge of where they came from, who they look like, what their earliest days and years were like. Every child deserves to know his or her own story. International adoption can make this more complicated, but it is still possible. Our process has not been perfect, but it has been good - for our daughter, and for us. We are not special people with special courage. If we can do it, with all the obstacles that sometimes stand in our way, it is possible for you, too.

Dealing With Questions When You Have No Answers

Erik Deckers

Erik Deckers is a professional writer, book author, and owner of a content marketing agency. He is the co-author of *Branding Yourself, No Bullshit Social Media,* and *The Owned Media Doctrine*. He is also a newspaper columnist and professional speaker. He and his wife Toni are the proud parents of three adopted children from Bolivia and Haiti, Maddie, Emma, and Ben.

* * *

We dealt with a lot of different questions, some rather rude or intrusive, when we were adopting our children. We are the proud parents of three children, one from Bolivia and two from Haiti, so our family would get a few stares, especially when we lived in small-town Indiana. And you can imagine the questions we got as we went through our process.

"What do your parents think?" ("About adopting black or Hispanic children" was left unsaid, for the most part. They were fine with it.)

"Are you going to have children of your own?" ("These are our own children," we said. "Do you mean 'biological children?'")

"Why there?" ("Why *not* there?")

In our own case, we adopted our kids because that was our first choice. We decided to go that route instead of having a biological child, but we still got all kinds of questions about fertility (especially my wife's! When people asked me about the fertility issue, it was always assumed that *I* was all kinds of fertile, but that *she* was the one with problems.)

Other times, we were asked about the international aspects, the process, and even the costs.

"What are the conditions of the orphanages like?"

"Did you get to choose your child?"

"How much did this set you back?"

There are times you won't know the answer to a question. There are times you won't want to answer the question. And there are some questions that people will ask, and you will gape at them, open-mouthed, wondering if you actually heard them say that. It is not that you can't answer, but it is more like you "can't even." But there are a few ways to deal with these questions when you have no answers. Or at least none you are allowed to share in polite society.

Humor Helps

Some questions are going to be rather (in)sensitive, and you can be offended and indignant, which will certainly put a strain on your relationship with the other person. Or, you can laugh it off with a smart aleck answer that will put both of you at ease and disarm any tension.

My three kids are from Bolivia and Haiti. Someone once asked me if we were going to tell our kids they were adopted.

"No," I said. "We're hoping they don't find out."

It was fun to watch the other person's face as they puzzled that one out. When they realized how silly my answer was, they understood that we would, of course, tell the kids they were adopted. But we both had a laugh, and I never had to answer a deeply personal question some people go their entire lives without revealing.

Be Honest

Just say "I don't know" or "I would rather not answer that." You can explain *why* you do not know, but if you do not have an answer, that is your answer. Feel free to share it. For example, we are often asked questions about our kids' birth parents. Since they were adopted from children's homes in their countries of origin, we do not actually know much about their lives before they arrived at the children's homes. So we have to say as much.

But, as someone who believes in adoption, we have also used this as a chance to educate the other person about what life is like for orphans and abandoned children and their parents in other countries. By explaining, even just a little bit, to someone else, I hope I am either planting a seed for further conversation, or at least creating a little more understanding about what the rest of the world is like.

LIE, IF YOU HAVE TO

I am not above lying if it is to protect my kids. There are just some questions that are no one's business and to ask them is rather rude. There are certain things we have not shared with our kids yet (see the section below, *"What If Your Kids Are Asking the Questions"*), and other things that they know, but we have all agreed not to share with other people. So I lie.

"I don't know," I'll tell someone when they ask about one of my kids' personal histories. "We never found out. I don't think anyone knows." Honesty is not always the best policy when people are digging into private family matters. Rather than make them feel stupid for asking, I just lie like it is my job.

BE DIRECT

Of course, some people do not like lying, and I don't blame you. So if you do not like lying to other people, don't do it. You can always tell them the truth, or you tell the other person, "I don't think that is any of your business," and then deal with the emotional conflict and the strain on the relationship, especially when it is your sweet old grandmother whose been a little confused lately and only asks questions because she wants to know more about your life. Lying is starting to looking pretty good now, huh?

Seriously though, there will be times where people just ask and ask and ask all kinds of questions about everything related to your adoption. It is one thing if you are having a conversation with someone else who is thinking about adopting a child. Those are people who want to know what they can expect in their own lives, because they are about to embark on your journey. But there are also people who just stick their nose into everything and have to know every salacious detail about other people's lives. This is where it is time to be direct and firm, but without actually trying to be rude. "I'm sorry, I am just not comfortable discussing this," you can tell them. "These are personal matters that we prefer to keep private." That is usually enough to tell the other person to stop with the questions.

WHAT IF YOUR PARENTS ARE ASKING THE QUESTIONS?

The above answers still apply. Unless you have both absolutely agreed you can share deeply personal information with your parents or in-laws, don't do it. Your children's feelings and privacy come first, even before your parents' curiosity. If you are old enough to adopt a

...d and have a family, you are old enough to talk to your parents like you are an adult.

WHAT IF YOUR KIDS ARE ASKING THE QUESTIONS?

This is a tough one, because your kids deserve to know nearly everything you know, but ultimately it comes down to when they are ready to know. When our kids were very young, we had two rules in our house whenever questions of sex came up. First, whenever one of them asked a question, we always asked "what do you mean?" so we could make sure we understood what they were asking. Second, we only answered the question they asked, without sharing more than they were ready for. That meant, if our three year old asked where babies came from, that was not the time to have the "when a man loves a woman very much" discussion. "Their mommy's tummy" was the best answer we could give. The time for the "other discussion" would come much later. But I have known parents who confused their child, because the kid only wanted to know "from her mommy's tummy," but instead got "first, you need a little wine and soft music."

So it goes with questions about adoption. When your child asks where they came from, or whether they are adopted, or why they were adopted, or any number of difficult questions, tailor it to their age and emotional state. First, ask them to clarify what they mean, so you know what they are really asking for. Second, answer only the question they asked. There will be plenty of time to explain more later. Do not overwhelm them with information, or you will only cause confusion and possible sadness or anger. You will have years to explain everything, so do not set them up for emotional problems later by oversharing with, or withholding from, your adopted child.

Finally, you absolutely have to understand the emotional health and well-being of your child. You have to know whether they can handle the answers you might tell them. I have heard horrific stories of abuse and neglect of children before they were adopted, as well as stories of rapes that led to pregnancy which led to adoptions. These are not stories to share with your child when they are young, or do not have the emotional strength to bear it. Make absolutely sure you know what your child can understand and can emotionally take before you share some of their deepest secrets with them.

Editor's note: Eventually, you will need to share with your child all that you know about his or her story. It is your child's story and therefore your child's story to know, to have, and to have control of. The general rule of thumb is full disclosure prior to the start of puberty, when emotional development requires full information to incorporate into identity development. While difficult truths may be hard to share, in general kids accept it better than parents anticipated. For more information on this topic, please refer to *Telling the Truth to Your Adopted or Foster Child* by Keefer and Schooler.

You are going to be asked all kinds of questions about your adoption, your child, and your family situation. People are naturally curious, and for the most part, their

are in the right place when they ask them. They are
asking out of spite or because they are terrible people.
They truly want to know.

If you are faced with a question you do not know how to
answer, your best bet is just to be honest and say, "I don't
know how to answer that," or "I prefer not to talk about
it." Other parents will say "that is his/her story to tell, not
mine" or even "why do you ask?" as a helpful response to
gently let people know they are being intrusive. People
will typically be respectful of your decision and honesty.

Part III

Therapists' Notes

Tough Questions: How to Talk About Adoption Issues with Your Child

Barbara Freedgood, LCSW

Barbara is an LCSW, licensed certified social worker, in the state of New York. She is a graduate of Fordham University School of Social Work, the NYU Post-Doctoral Training in Marriage and Family Therapy and Joyce Maguire Pavao's Adoption Certification Training. She has been a therapist in private practice since 1980. She has written and presented internationally on infertility and adoption issues. She runs support groups for adoptive parents and is the mother of two children, who are now adults, she adopted at birth in the United States. Her blog, Ruminations on Adoption can be found on her website: *www.barbarafreedgood.com*

* * *

The adoptive parent's role is especially challenging because they have to introduce very complex truths to a child and then be prepared to support him-even to stay a step ahead-as he makes sense of the truths of his life.
~ Joyce Maguire

ADOPTIVE PARENTS HAVE TO ANSWER TOUGH QUESTIONS

I was recently asked to speak to a group of adoptive parents on the topic of "how to answer the hard questions regarding adoption." I was given a list of questions in advance in the hope that I would have the answers to them by the time I arrived to give my presentation. As I read through the questions I was struck by a number of things. First, the way in which we are thinking about adoption has changed so dramatically in recent years from closed to open. Second, for many questions, there is no one right or easy answer. And lastly, how very much the adoptive parent has to metabolize for their child in order to help them make some sense of their story.

Explaining adoption and all the back story that it involves is one of the most challenging jobs that parents who have adopted are required to do to support the wholeness of their children. It is no easy task and it requires some deep and unselfish soul searching. Most certainly it involves relinquishing the notion that adoption forms a family like any other. In fact it is a way of forming a family that is unlike any other and one that requires parents to face questions and challenges that are far outside the range of biological families.

...en the case with adoptive parents, I arrived to
. filled with people who were eager to share the joy
.aving found their children and the pain of trying to
manage the many challenges they were encountering.
Challenges, I might add, that no one prepared them for in
advance. Questions included: "How do I tell my child
that he has siblings who were not placed for adoption?"
"How and when do I explain the one child policy in
China to my children before they discover it on the
internet?" "What do I say when my child asks if they can
go to live with their birth family?" "I had an open
adoption and the birth mother has disappeared. What do I
tell my child?" "We don't know anything about the birth
father. What do I tell my child?"

Of course the right answer is that you must tell your child
the truth as you know it. Anything less than the truth
about their adoption is a betrayal of trust, as any adult
adopted person will tell you. The question in adoption is
how do you give your child the truth in ways they can
digest? How do you answer such big questions that
contain so much complexity when a child's cognitive and
emotional development is not up to understanding? The
answer is that you answer slowly over time, layering
nuance as a child develops to be able to comprehend
complexity and metabolize the many emotions this
engenders. For this task you need a framework to be able
to gage what is appropriate at what age and you need the
skills to keep the dialogue open with your child. Easier
said than done!

There are two different and fundamental ways in which a
parent needs to be prepared to discuss adoption issues
with their child. They are of course interrelated. In

addition to all the usual roles that any parent fulfills for a child, your job as an adoptive parent is to explain to your child that they are adopted and to give them their story. The second task will follow upon the first. You will have to answer all the questions that follow. This is not a linear process, nor one that happens in one or two conversations. It unfolds over time and in unanticipated moments. You can tell your child something about their adoption and hear nothing from them about it for months at a time. Then one day, when you least expect it, a question will come. I have found these moments have happened with my own children when we are driving or walking or doing some other activity that involves not being we face-to-face. Looking directly at me when asking these questions seems to be too much, which gives us some idea of how hard it is for the child to ask.

At these moments you are called upon to summon up all the information and advice you have ever heard about adoption, take a deep breath, synthesize it in less than a minute and reply. It is usually not a leisurely conversation with lots of time and space around it. It is a moment in time when a window opens and you need to be ready, ready to say something true, something understanding, and something safe. You are mentally multi-tasking at the speed of light before the window shuts and the risk your child has taken to ask you a hard question gives way to closing again. Keeping it open long enough to connect and let them know you are there to answer these questions and help them understand them is the job you have taken on. You have to manage your own feelings, figure out the right thing to say and above all, take care of their feelings to the best of your ability. There are no auditions or rehearsals. You're on!

ん

, ou can always return to a subject. You can
as best you can and promise to give something
thought and get back to your child with more of an
swer if you are really stumped. *Make sure you make
good on your promises.* Your child is tracking to see if it
is safe to ask what he or she wants to know. If you drop
it, it sends a signal that they should too. Like all children,
adopted children will protect their parents from anything
they think will hurt them. If your child feels that
questions about their adoption will upset you, they will
make the decision not to ask, and it will churn inside of
them and come out in other, less desirable ways such as
depression, acting out behaviors, poor performance at
school, etc.

A FRAMEWORK FOR THINKING ABOUT HOW TO ANSWER THE TOUGH QUESTIONS

All children ask difficult questions and all parents have to
deal with answering them. However, adoptive parents
have to deal with answering children's questions about
their origins. The questions they ask have the potential to
undermine the basis of their security. Furthermore, the
person they want to ask, their parent, is also the
relationship that can be most threatened by these
questions. This is why it is so important that we, as
parents, do our own work within ourselves before we
speak with our children. We must investigate our own
feelings and reactions to information before asking them
to do that same work. Otherwise we place an unfair
burden on them to sort out material that we ourselves are
unclear about. That said, no one is perfect and it is a

messy job filled with unexpected twists and turns. You have to aim for doing the very best you can and know that sometimes, you may fall short. Every parent does sometimes.

In order to speak to your child about adoption you need to hold in mind simultaneously several threads. How old are they and what is their developmental stage? What is the cognitive level of this age? What are they able to process and understand? And then, how will the issue affect them emotionally as they feel the impact of the information you give them, and how can you best be aware of and tend to these feelings - both theirs and your own?

The idea of "holding in mind" or "mentalizing" is a concept in the field of relational psychology that provides a useful idea for thinking about how to talk to children about adoption. Mentalizing is the simple but essential ability to understand the mental state of oneself and others. This is one of the most critical functions of a parent. It represents the ability to reflect back to your child their reality, something we all need to not feel crazy. The psychologist Peter Fonagy did extensive research into the critical role of mentalizing in successful attachment and parenting. He found that psychopathology can develop when there is a failure on the part of the parents to mentalize the experience of the child which is why it is so critically important that we work to understand our children, both adopted and biological.

For adoptive parents, mentalizing our children's experience requires a huge leap out of ourselves and into the shoes of another whose experience we do not share, unless the parent is also adopted. It also involves the painful process of allowing into our own consciousness the struggles our children face. It is common to want to feel that by adopting we have solved a problem, given a child a secure, loving home. It is hard to admit that, with the solution of adoption, come the problems of adoption. The gain entails a loss. It is challenging to be required as an adoptive parent to imagine the feelings of loss, confusion and disorientation an adopted child must encounter as they grasp the meaning of adoption, however loved and secure they may feel in the family that has adopted them.

As Kerrie Seigl has outlined in the next chapter, there are two other very useful theories of development that are helpful for thinking about what age children are able to understand information. These are the cognitive theory of Jean Piaget and the psychological stages of development proposed by Erik Erikson. They each describe normal cognitive and emotional development for children in general. In addition to the developmental milestones that every child has to pass through to achieve maturity, the adopted child will also experience the "Seven Core Issues of Adoption" as originally defined by researchers Silverstein and Kaplan. These include: loss, rejection, guilt and shame, grief, identity, intimacy, and mastery and control. To assist parents with the task of thinking about how to speak to their child about adoption, please refer to the chart on page 272-273 to observe how these issues can interface and co-occur. This provides a framework to continue to think about how to talk to your child about adoption and how to answer their questions by serving as a guidepost to remember what is appropriate to their age and stage, while also holding in mind the emotions that may accompany their growing understanding of their story.

While development of cognitive and emotional functions happens fairly predictably according to the work of both Piaget and Erikson, the seven core issue of adoption can occur at any age and in no particular order, often reappearing thematically throughout one's life. They create an undertow that is part of the landscape of adoption. As they grow and mature, children's increasing awareness of what adoption means increases their vulnerability to these seven core feelings. Additionally their interaction with the world and how other people react to this fact of their lives contributes to these feelings being triggered at different moments by different things. A parent who knows this is more able to think about the fact that, what may look like inexplicable behavior actually has very good reasons and and may in fact be grief over the losses of adoption and the terrible reality of not feeling wanted or being kept by a birth family. A few thoughtful questions can allow these feelings to be okay. The worst mistake an adoptive parent can make is to feel hurt or take personally their child's adoption grief. As indicated in the title of this anthology, "**it's not about you.**"

How to Talk About Adoption to Your Child at Different Ages and Stages

Now that I have outlined what the work of the adoptive parent is with regard to answering the tough questions and some guidelines for thinking about it, here is how to do it. To begin, look at the first task of the adoptive parent with regard to talking to their child about adoption. Before answering the many questions that will arise over the course of your life with your child, first you have to tell your child that they are adopted and what that means. You have to give them the general information and then you have to tell them their own unique story to the best of your knowledge and as best you can.

The current wisdom is that the term "adoption" and the fact that children are adopted should be a part of language from the beginning, even though the actual meaning cannot be understood. As language begins to emerge, the word "adoption" is introduced through stories. The term gets introduced by explaining that it is a way of forming a family, emphasizing that it is forever and that the baby acts just like any baby—in short, the idea is to normalize it in the best sense.

How does this look? What do you say and when? I had a mother come to me guilt-ridden that she had not talked enough to her three year old about being adopted. The social worker she used while she was adopting had counseled her to tell her child she was adopted from the very beginning, but she neglected to give her much guidance on what to say and how to say it. If you look at the above chart, you see that the child between two and five years old is what Piaget calls a pre-operational thinker. They are able to make cause and effect leaps, but are not able to make logical meaning of things. They are not able to understand the meaning of what adoption is, but they can hear the word and understand by your tone and repetition that it applies to them. The point of letting them know this from the time they have words is so that later, when they begin to grasp what it actually means, it is not a complete surprise. It is something they have already heard. What is actually means will feel new though as they begin to understand it.

There are many wonderful children's books about adoption. The website www.tapestry.com is a wonderful resource for current titles. Books on adoption for young children are a great way of introducing adoption to them. They usually include the idea that adoption is a way of forming a family and it is forever. This can be discussed when you read the book. You can simply tell your child *I or we adopted you and that is how we became a family.* A popular term is to refer to family as "forever family" reinforcing the idea that adoption is forever. (Editors note: *I like the term "no matter what family" for several reasons. "Forever" can be ominous, even threatening for a child feeling confused about their own feelings about adoption. Forever also cannot really be promised. "No matter what" also directly responds to the fears of re-relinquishment. If the story is that the birth mother did not have the money to care for a child, the child may fear abandonment if the adoptive mother loses her job. "No matter what" takes on the tone of "till death do us part" and is more concrete than "forever".)*

The young child will not understand much more than this, so if you begin to try to tell them a lot more, they can be overwhelmed. You may also think that they understand more than they do since they may parrot what you have told them without really comprehending the meaning of it. For example, one child, when asked about his family reported, "My mother is a doctor, my father is a teacher and I'm 'dopted." They understand that everybody is assigned a category, but the difference between categories is unclear.

It is not until the age of five or so, when children want to know where babies come from, that the meaning of adoption really "comes out of the closet." Consider the distortions that young children of this age come up with when they hear about how "Daddy plants a seed in Mommy." In The Magic Years, Fraiberg (1959, p. 193) discusses children's cognitive processing of the information about where they came from. Given the story about the father planting a seed in the mother, one child imagines that the mother swallows it and another thinks the doctor takes it out of the father and puts it in the mother. When told the story of adoption, many children conclude that all children are adopted and that that is how babies come into families. They are born to someone else and Mommy and Daddy come to pick them up.

When I explained the story of his adoption to my five year old son, he put his hands over his ears and said, "Tell me again." When he inquired why his birthmother made an adoption plan for him, I told him that she could not take care of him, and she wanted him to have parents who could. When pressed on why, I told him she was very poor. Revealing this same cognitive level of children grappling with reproduction, he asked, "Why didn't she go to the bank and get some money?"

It is useful to be aware of common fantasies that adopted children report regarding being relinquished for adoption. In an attempt to gain mastery and control over their situation, they often imagine it is due to some defect in themselves, that they are somehow unlovable or are the wrong sex (Brodzinsky, Schecter, & Marantz, 1992, p. 95). Another fantasy is that they were stolen or kidnapped, thus undoing the possibility that it was a conscious choice on the part of their birthparents, protecting them from their rage at the abandonment (Hodges, 1984). Here you see some of the seven core issues coming out: feelings of loss, rejection, grief, shame and a wish for mastery and control over the entire experience.

The world-altering information of what being adopted actually means is something the adopted child and adoptive family are dealing with from the point at which you tell your child their story onward, whether it is openly discussed or not. Parents may assume that children are not interested if they do not bring it up. In *Twenty Things Adopted Children Wish Their Parents Knew*, Eldridge (1999, p. 85) encourages parents to start conversations about adoption that signal to their children that it is okay to talk about it. Without this encouragement, children are more likely to go underground with their feelings, only to have them surface negatively later.

This point was brought home to me when I attended a lecture given by the director of the Spence-Chapin Adoption Agency. The agency runs workshops for parents and children. They separate parents and children into different rooms. In the parents' group they asked, "Does your child talk about adoption?"

The parents, to a person, replied, "No."

In the room with the children, they asked do you think about your birth families? Almost every child replied, "Yes."

This gives us some important information and some clues for how to speak to children about adoption. If you ask them about whether or not they are thinking about "adoption" they may say nothing. It is an abstract concept that they can only begin to think about as they get older. However, if you ask them if they think about their birth families, you will get more information. This can be done in simple, matter-of-fact ways. For example, my daughter once remarked that we do not have the same hair. I asked her if she wished she had hair like me. She replied, "No, I wish you had hair like mine!" Here is an opportunity to wonder together. "I bet you have hair like your birth mother or father. What do you think?" It is simple and concrete. Remember, the child of five to eight is a master of the concrete.

Creating a safe space for children to ask their questions and discuss what they are thinking about their adoption story is challenging for adoptive parents. Sometimes, in an effort to not upset themselves and their children, parents make the mistake of delivering very difficult information in too casual a manner. This leaves their children with the disconnect of having heard something mind-altering delivered in a matter-of-fact tone that does not match the experience it causes the child to have.

I encountered an example of this when I consulted with some parents who had something very difficult to tell their daughter. They had discovered that she had a different birth father than the one she had been told she had and with whom she had been having a relationship with in an open adoption. In their struggle to deal with the shock of this information and wanting to protect their child from this shock, the parents were imagining telling their daughter in a casual way that the man she had been thinking was her birth father was not. Rather than preparing their daughter by letting her know they had something big to tell her, they were trying on the possibility of just saying, "You know it turns out that Bill is not your birthfather." With the best of intentions to downplay a very confusing and big piece of information, they were risking leaving their child feeling quite alone with too much to understand.

On a lighter note, my daughter announced to me one day, "I bet I got my sense of fashion from my birthmother." This, I must admit was a blow, as I consider myself to have a pretty good sense of fashion and felt quite sure that it was me she got it from. Here is another moment when the adoptive parent is required to shelve the feelings of jealousy or competition and enter the arena of imagining together what qualities and fantasies the child has about birth origins and inherited qualities. This connects them to their roots, but also connects them to you by allowing the space to be safe for these speculations. Of course in an open adoption more is known about inherited qualities. However, there is always room for imagining things and testing the waters of whether or not it is safe for the adopted child to be open about it and integrate all parts of themselves.

As the child's social world expands beyond the family when they go to school, new issues begin to present themselves, such as how to talk to teachers, parents, and other children about adoption. Their cognitive level leads their peers to express to the adopted child a hurtful deduction: "Your real mother gave you up because she didn't love you." No matter what carefully chosen words you have given your child to help ease the pain of her adoption, their friends will give them the brutal truth-as-they-see-it. Parents are left to manage the damage, but they may not even know it has occurred because the child will try to protect the parents by not telling them.

The feelings and fear that they were rejected by birthparents because something was wrong or unlovable about them is further complicated by the fact that many adopted children do have very real neurological difficulties. In addition to genetic or prenatal factors, there is also the question of what component of the adopted population presenting as learning disabled or behaviorally impaired are suffering from relational trauma due to adoption-related loss that prompts dissociative reactions, which impair concentration and focus (Bromberg, 2011; Pavao, 2005). In these cases, the notion that one was abandoned by the original mother because one was bad or defective is only given greater traction by the reality that many of these children are truly suffering from varying degrees of neurological damage or trauma.

During the elementary school years adoptive parents need to be on the lookout for behavior that may indicate something upsetting has occurred at school that your child may not tell you. I remember one evening my daughter was being particularly impossible and I could not understand what had gotten into her. In the third or fourth explosion of the evening I asked her, "Is something the matter?" It tumbled out of her. "Susie asked my why my real mother didn't't keep me!" She then fell into my arms sobbing.

How do we talk to our children about these awful moments and how do we handle them? First, we mentalize and empathize. "That must have felt absolutely awful! Let's talk about it when you calm down. First of all, you have two real mothers. You have a mother who gave birth to you, and you have a mother who is raising you. Both are real mothers." Again, this is very concrete and it is true. Giving birth makes you a mother and adopting and raising a child makes you a mother. "You can tell your friend that your birth mother was not able to take care of a baby when you were born and she wanted you to have a mother who could. Your mother who is raising you is your real mother too." This is hard stuff. There is no way to make it easy, but if you can make it simple and concrete you can give your child the tools to manage. Other children usually do not mean to be hurtful with their questions. If anything, the idea of adoption is probably scary to them. The notion of a mother not being able to take care of their child is scary for a child. What if that happened to their mother too?

Not all adoptive mothers do want to refer to the birth mother as a mother. They want to feel that they are the only mother. It can be confusing to everyone to say you have two mothers. The point of the above paragraph is to put the focus on the fact that a birth mother is real and an adoptive mother is a real mother as well. The birthmother did part of the mother job by carrying and bringing your child into the world. The rest of the time you will refer to her as a birth mother, first mother, or whatever term your family has decided they are comfortable with using.

While the struggle with the meaning of adoption simmers to varying degrees during the elementary school years, it explodes in preadolescence and adolescence. During this developmental period of identity formation and differentiation, the adopted child and family carry a double burden. They are passing through a life stage that is tumultuous in any family; however, they are expected to master it similarly to any family, only once again, they are reminded of their invisible wounds.

There are a number of tasks that are developmentally required at this age that are complicated by adoption. Adolescence is a time of existential angst when most teenagers typically struggle to form their identity and leave home to launch into the world. Again we see one of the seven core adoption issues: identity. It is a time of a second birth, of pushing out of the womb of the home out into life on one's own. For the adopted child this is particularly difficult. It can happen that they fail at things to prove it was inevitable that they were rejected by their birthparents. They struggle not wanting to leave the home that took them in when they were rejected. They often rage quietly in their rooms, broadcasting their outsider status in loud silence, or they act out wildly. They can enact their experience of feeling rejected by their birth mother by rejecting themselves (Fairbairn, 1943). They often test to see if now, after all this time, their parents will finally abandon them. They pull out all the stops, and parents are left whipping in the wind of this emotional roller coaster.

During this stage of adolescence the parents of adopted children are challenged to contain an emotional tornado and to try to prevent it from wreaking too much destruction. And it is the parents' task to contain their own grief and bewilderment as well as that of their child. How successful parents are in containing this tornado depends heavily on the support and permission they receive to have their feelings without shame and guilt. Parents need to be supported to hold the truth of their struggle as well as the love born out of the attachment to their children at the same time in order to allow the love to triumph.

During adolescence, when young adoptees are struggling to launch in the world (Brodazinsky, 1992, p. 101; Pavao, 2005, p. 39), adoptive parents can relive earlier anxieties similar to those associated with their infertility if that is what they experienced before adopting. While the children of their peers may be more able to leave the nest, adoptive parents once again live with a sense of otherness, perhaps of failure and certainly disappointment that their lives and their children's lives are not progressing in a "normal" way. Adopted children may develop more slowly, needing more time at home to be able to leave. When they finally do, the gratification can be all the more satisfying. If parents can understand that these issues are at play during the adolescence of their adopted children it can help withstand the hurt and bewilderment that occurs when, believing that you have done at least a decent job of being a parent, your child seems hell bent on proving otherwise.

How to Think About and Answer Tough Questions Kids Ask About Their Adoptions

Thus far I have discussed the trajectory of development from early childhood through adolescence and what some of the key issues are in discussing adoption with your child as they mature and develop. Along the way, the tough questions will surface. Each question is an opportunity to discover more about your child and to grow together. Do not assume you know what your child is asking when the questions come. Stay curious. Ask them what they mean, what they want to know. By way of illustrating this idea, I will share some of the questions that I mentioned were posed to me at the presentation I spoke of in the beginning of this chapter. Examples can be the best illustration of concepts that you can apply to any question.

Some questions can be more jarring that others. One that is high on the scale of jolting inquiries is one I mentioned earlier: "Can I go live with my birth family?" A parent has to manage an avalanche of their own feelings to achieve the moment when they can be curious about the meaning of such a question. At first pass, it feels like total rejection for an adoptive parent. But if we can stop long enough to think and wonder what the child is asking, we may reach a very different conclusion. It is possible, for example, that it really means "Will you let me go too?" Or it can be a chance to explore their fantasy of what it might be like to live with their birth family.

Once you have allowed the feeling that comes with such a question, you can always start with a simple response: "What do you think that would be like?" Often children imagine that in the birth family home they might have the "perfect" family we all wish for that has no rules and lets us do whatever we want. That could be one fantasy. Another possible answer is that they might not have such a great time and that they might miss you. You have no idea what your child imagines about these things unless you make the space for them to tell you. The more you do, the closer you will be!

The questions regarding why a child was placed and siblings were not is another extremely challenging one. Of course any parent worries about how hurtful this will feel for their child. The dilemma is, if we are telling our children the truth and the truth is so painful, how and when do we give them this information. A child might be able to understand cognitively, but psychologically the information could be completely overwhelming. When we are psychologically overwhelmed one defense mechanism we can deploy is dissociation. An example of this is a mother with whom I spoke who told me she had told her son about siblings that were with his birthmother and that he had gone blank and had not retained the information. This is a way of signaling that a he was not ready or able to integrate the information.

This is one reaction, but there is also the possibility that the information will be met with curiosity and relief at having the whole truth. In an open adoption of course the child is able to meet these siblings and have relationships with them. In a closed adoption there is more unknown to process and this can be handled, as I have outlined before, with wondering out loud about it and what the circumstances were that lead to the placement of your child and not the others, emphasizing that it was not the child's fault but a difficult circumstance that lead a birth parent to want them to have a home where they could be better taken care of and raised.

In the current climate of openness and sharing of information, there are difficult decisions like these that parents are faced with making about what to tell when. It may be that a child cannot handle information and that you have to wait to tell them when they are a bit older. It is a catch twenty-two. Either way they will have feelings of hurt, anger, and betrayal and either way you, as the parent, will be faced with fielding their reactions. If we are trying to avoid our children's anger or pain, we do well to remember that all parents have to tolerate their children's anger, set limits and make decisions about what is going to best facilitate their integration as people. And while **it is not about you,** you have to gage as a parent what you can manage and how you can best manage it. In the end your child will benefit the most from a parent who is able to mentalize their own mental state and capacity as well as that of their child. For this we need to pay careful attention to ourselves as well as our children. In the end, this is the way to do our best on the mind-expanding journey of raising our children who have come to us through adoption.

References

Brodzinsky, D. M.; Schecter, M. D.; & Henig, R. M. (1992). *Being Adopted.* New York City, NY: Doubleday.

Bromberg, P. A. (2011). *Standing in the Spaces: Essays on clinical process trauma and dissociation.* Abingdon, UK: Routledge.

Eldridge, S. (1999). *Twenty Things Adopted Kids Wish Their Adoptive Parents Knew.* Crystal Lake, IL: Delta.

Fairbairn, W. R. D. (1943). The repression and the return of the bad objects. In *Psychoanalytic Studies of the Personality,* pp. 59-81, London: Tavistock, 1952.

Fraiberg, S. H. (1996). *The Magic Years: Understanding and handling the problems of early childhood.* New York, NY: Scribner. Hodges, 1984

Pavao, J. M. (2005). *The Family of Adoption: Completely revised and updated.* Boston, MA: Beacon Press.

Core Adoption Issues	Psycho-Social Stages	Cognitive Stages	Age Expectations
Rejection Suffers fear of abandonment and feelings of not being good enough to stay with	**Trust vs. Mistrust** Infant develops a sense of trust that he/she will be cared for or feels unsafe and thus general mistrust	**Sensorimotor** Coordination of senses with motor response. Language used for demands and cataloguing	0-18 months
Loss Child has trouble holding on and letting go	**Autonomy vs. Shame** Begins to develop self-control and independence or feels ashamed of desire to explore the world separate from the primary caregiver		18 months - 2 years
		Pre-Operational Symbolic thinking, use of proper syntax and grammar to express concepts.	2-3 years
Guilt and Shame Believes he/she does not deserves good fortune and struggles with anger Guilt is "I did something bad" v. Shame is "I am bad."	**Initiative vs. Guilt** Begins to develop personal power, agency or feels guilt when ideas do not turn out as he/she expected		3-5 years
	Industry vs. Inferiority Navigates social world and school where recognition is based on skill or feels inferior if he/she cannot perform as desired		5-7 years
		Concrete Operational Concepts attached to concrete situations. Time, space and quantity are understood and can be applied, but not as independent concepts	7-11 years

Core Adoption Issues		Cognitive Stages	Age Expectations
Identity Grapples with integrating all parts of himself. Who am I? Where did I come from?		**Formal Operations** Theoretical, hypothetical, abstract logic and reasoning. Strategy and planning become possible Concepts learned in one context can be applied to another.	11-12 years
	Ego Identity vs. Role Confusion Develops sense of personal identity or feels confusion if unable to.		Adolescence
Intimacy May bond inappropriately-too soon, too late, too intensely, not at all-because fears loss, abandonment, rejection	**Intimacy vs. Isolation** Forms intimate relationships or feels isolated if cannot.		Early adulthood
Mastery and Control Realizing what adoption has done to him/her, feels powerless and seeks what control he/she can find	**Generativity vs. Stagnation** Becomes a productive adult or stagnates. Has a drive to leave a positive impact on the world and/or younger generations		Middle adulthood
Grief Unresolved Grief can lead to depression and anger	**Ego Integrity vs. Despair** Achieves a sense of accomplishment and satisfaction with life or feels despair. Ego integrity is an acceptance of the way things have been and despair is anger and/or fear of death		Late adulthood

Developing One's Self-Concept from Conception

Kerrie Byrnes Siegl, LMFT

While obtaining her Bachelor's Degree in Child Development from Purdue University, Kerrie became passionate about the unique differences in people based on their life experiences, family history, and biological make-up. Kerrie graduated with a Masters in Marriage and Family Therapy from the Christian Theological Seminary of Indianapolis. Kerrie works in private practice seeing child, teens and adults with a variety of mental health and relational issues. She is driven to help individuals and families learn to develop healthy relationships and help people of all ages uncover their strengths and discover their own abilities to find healing. She is passionate about children who have been adopted and are trying to attach to their caregivers. She worked for Bethany Christian Services as an adoption therapist obtaining training in several attachment modalities, and then moved on to work in community mental health in the school systems with children in K-12. She has worked in a variety of mental health settings including home based services with foster care children, adoption services (home and school), school-based and home based services to low-income families in Central Indiana. Kerrie is married and has two young children. She is active in her local church and other community activities.

* * *

Whether a child is adopted at birth or later into development, all children will have to develop a sense of self-concept. While this concept continues to develop throughout children's life changes, experiences, and relationships, it starts from the moment of conception as a child attaches in the womb to their mother. And even if only for those forty-weeks, a child still starts to experience life, attachment, love and a sense of who they are from their experiences; it is the foundation for their self-concept. Walking through each stage of development from conception to young adulthood, children learn to figure out who they are by the information and stories given to them. For children that have been adopted, not only is an adoption story important, but the birth family, their culture, history, and relationships are essential for the child to discover all the pieces of who they are. When children are not given these pieces, when they do not have access to those pieces because of lack of information given to the adoptive family, or when children are denied those pieces due to the stance of the adoptive parents, a child can struggle to feel fully self-confident in their identity.

CONCEPTION AND EARLY INFANCY

Attachment theory researchers have started to discover scientific evidence that shows fetal stress is related to the early attachment between a mother and their child. While it is harder to measure an infant's experience in the womb, scientists now use the heart rates of infants to show how various stimuli affect an infant's experience (Lewis, Amini, & Lannon, 2000). This has dramatically changed the way the modern world delivers and treats newborn infants and strongly influences their medical care and nutrition in the first few days of life. Often, for children that are adopted, the birth experience is not always a process that promotes secure attachment. The various factors which contribute to a mother choosing adoption for her child (poverty, lack of nourishment, emotional and mental stress, physical traumas, substance abuse, etc.) will have a profound impact on the child's brain development and attachment. Additionally, sometimes these women are unable to bond with their child at birth for a variety of reasons, often outside of their control.

In their studies, researchers noted that children who were removed from their mother at delivery had higher heart rates than those who were immediately placed with skin to skin care, indicating distress (Bergman, Linley, and Fawcus, 2004). For a child who is immediately removed, a sense of stress starts in the infant as their instincts to find food and safety are interrupted by separation. These heart rates remained higher for infants in the study until they were able to find food and touch. If this is a child's first experience in the world, a sense of anxiety and lack of safety have set the stage and future expectations. Some researchers have identified that infants are so attuned to their mother's voice and sound, that they can tell who their mother is by the way the newborns body displays stress cues like rooting for her breast or turning their head toward her voice. When proper bonding and attachment occur, it sets the stage for a child to develop within our "normal" ranges (Harlow, 1959). Normal is a relative term because there is no perfect attachment, but rather a continuum of attachments from secure, insecure, avoidant, and disorganized.

In my work as a therapist, some children who I have worked with who had infant adoptions from South Korea noted a sense of unknown anxiety. When processing their birth and adoption story, they identified with the fear and anxiety an infant would have experienced being transferred from birth mother, medical staff, social worker, foster family, riding a plane to the U.S for twelve hours or more, and finally being placed with their adoptive family who looked, smelled, and spoke differently than anything they had ever experienced. This process is often extended over several months of time, and children would start to form attachments with foster families and then would be transitioned to their forever family. Sometimes this process occurred over the first six to twelve months of their lives, and for some, the process lingered well into their second year of life. It was unclear if their birth families ever got to spend any time with them and what their initial months of life were like. Most have little to no information about their birth story, birth families, or the foster families who cared for them.

Some of these children, despite being very attached to their adoptive families said things like, "I just always felt like I didn't belong or fit in" or "I just have never felt calm". This lack of security and identity were further affirmed by later experiences in the family. The adoptive parents of these children reported, "they were always kind of nervous, clingy, and never seemed ok on their own". They discussed trying to love these children more intentionally, but struggled to find the ability to soothe the child even from the first moments they were trying to bond with them. While some were able to slowly attach, most still report an underlying sense of things not feeling safe, especially when normal life events occur. By using the birth story and trying to piece together the emotions that started their journey, these young adults gathered a sense of acceptance for their sense of feeling detached. One young man was able to describe a new sense of acceptance about his anxiety and identity issues by saying, "just thinking about what that must have been like makes a lot of sense about why I feel the way I do today".

EARLY CHILDHOOD

Children grow at such a rapid rate in their first three years, that many have already developed a personality, attachment style, and have started their journey of developing their sense of self. In toddlerhood, children start to pull away from their caregivers and form a sense of self through a series of relational interactions. This is why so many typical developing children at eighteen months start to say "no" and "mine". They have started to realize they are their own person and are capable of trying to do what they want to do. Also by this age, behavioral issues start to arise for children who are not attaching properly. The continuum system, Attachment theory, is the joint work of John Bowlby and Mary Ainsworth (Ainsworth & Bowlby, 1991). The theory, which has been researched and developed since the 1940's, shows how a child requires a "secure base" from which to explore the world. Children without this base explore the world much differently, much more emotionally, and much less intentionally. This traumatic style of living and growing has an impact on learning, development, future relationships, and a child's emotional wellbeing. Children who are adopted in this stage of development can repair an attachment, but also struggle with allowing a parent to comfort them when they are upset, may be angry with a caregiver for leaving for even just small periods of time, and may require and extensive amount of consoling and soothing to re-regulate their emotions.

Often this secure base can be repaired by an adoptive family. Through attachment-based therapies and parenting methods which focus on the emotional age of the child opposed to the chronological age of the child, a child can attach to a parent figure. While this process takes time and often feels like the child is emotionally behind, it allows for healing to take place for the child as both their biological attachment figures and adoptive caregivers take on new roles for them, and the adoptive parent and child dyad attempt to start a more secure path from which to develop. The more severely detached or insecurely attached a child is to their previous caregivers is also affected by the duration of that attachment, additional traumas experienced by the child, and neglect issues (i.e. being emotionally isolated, children who went extended periods of time being distressed without a parent response, children who had little to no touch or parent/child interaction, or children who were not getting proper nutrition). This is why many attachment therapies focus on feeding, nurturing, setting structure, playing and touching a child as these were missed opportunities during infancy the child needed to experience to develop a bond and attachment with their parent. These are the building blocks of attachment.

There are two main theorists who discuss the brain development that occurs at this time that will help adoptive families understand what is occurring for their children that I will explain in more detail in this chapter. When one of these areas of development does not occur as planned, this is typically where emotional and behavioral problems start to occur. If a child cannot make sense of the world in which they live, they might start to feel scared, angry, unsafe, worried, or simply check out to the world around them as a way to stay safe. These basic instincts are for survival: physically and emotionally.

Jean Piaget was one of the first early childhood development scientists. In his work, he developed a four stage theory on how children think and learn based on how they engage in the world around them with objects. By the time a child enter school, they realize that objects in the world have meaning from people, toys, pets, and television figures. Those meanings are based on the child's emotions and relationships from their life experiences. By the time children would go to middle school, they have learned how these symbols operate and can transcend concrete thinking and situations.

As related to caregiving, parents are considered "objects" who have meaning. They become symbols that are good, bad, or somewhere in between. An absent father may have no meaning at all. An abusive mother may be both good and nurturing when she provides food, but bad and scary when she overreacts and hits the child for exploring their world. Parents who are using drugs or alcohol often have complicated meanings for children as the parent's mood can vary so much during times of use and sobriety. When children are little, their parent's identity is usually more rigid and simple. This is why children placed into foster care often idealize their missing parent figure despite being exposed to violence and negligence. For a child to have a secure attachment, they would need to have at least one consistent good object who is providing the necessary care for the child. Since parents can provide care on a continuum of levels with a variety of strengths and weaknesses, it is easy to see how then the attachment to that object.

For a child who does not get proper play and development experiences from their caregiver, symbols either do not have meaning, they have improper meaning, or their ability to construct consistency never develops. This can explain children with disorganized attachment styles who might seek love and affection but will often report feeling unsafe with adults. Adults have various meanings to this child due to their previous life experience. The more extreme the experiences that the child has with their world, the more confusing the world becomes. They have learned that adults are un predictable and unsafe, yet, the child craves to be cared for by an adult.

When children know more about their adoption story, they can later learn that their complex and often conflicting feelings were likely due to parents who were unable to provide appropriate care. Children can learn about how issues like poverty, mental illness, addictions, and lack of education about appropriate child rearing practices can make a loving parent feel scary or unsafe. When secure and safe attachment figures externalize why adults might be seen confusing or scary to the child, the child can start to see the more complex ways of thinking that "all parents are not safe, but some are".

An adopted child from Central America lived with her mother and at times with her grandmother. Her mother was an alcoholic who was frequently violent and had strange men over to their house who hurt the child. The grandmother was also physically abusive, but she seemed to be very consistent in her routine as she worked in a market and was able to provide some for their family. The child was adopted around five years of age and in telling her story she often referred to her mother as "bad" and her grandmother as "good". The adoptive family was very confused about how even though the child was beaten by her grandmother for not selling enough items in the market, the child saw her as "such a good grandma". The child transferred the attachment to grandmas to her adoptive family's grandparents but rejected the adoptive mother. In processing the child's experience we realized she never felt nurtured, loved, or cared for by her mother, but she did at least get structure, consistency, and some provision from her grandma. From the outside looking in, both birth family caregivers were abusive, unloving, and unsafe for the child, but the child had a mixed experience with her grandmother and even felt like she was "good" in comparison because she at least knew what to expect from her grandmother. This later translated to the child saying in therapy, "I like grandmas because they are nice, but I don't want to have a mom". For this child, having a mother was scary and unpredictable, but grandmas were a better provider (a good object). Her life story, had it not been processed from her lens, would have been quite confusing as to why she could be open to give two new grandmothers a chance to love her but not a new mother.

Another influential social scientist, Erik Erikson, created a more expansive eight stage theory on the stages of psychosocial development. The stages in the table below are created to represent "normal" developing children and the stages that correlate. "According to the theory, successful completion of each stage results in a healthy personality and the acquisition of basic virtues. Basic virtues are characteristic strengths which the ego can use to resolve subsequent crises. Failure to successfully complete a stage can result in a reduced ability to complete further stages and therefore a more unhealthy personality and sense of self. These stages, however, can be resolved successfully at a later time" (McLeod, 2013). Erikson's stages describe a ripple effect for developing children when it comes to their value structures and identity. It shows that each stage builds off the others. Understanding the stages of this theory and finding out where a child is currently developing is essential to knowing where to help them start their journey of creating a self-concept.

Please refer to the chart prior to this chapter on page 282-283. A child's therapist should be assessing what stage a child is developing at rather than what age they are based on their birth date. A child that has been adopted who is functioning like a toddler is going to be engaging in constant power struggles. He or she will be trying to assert their own will but can learn the balance between their will and their parent's will. If a child is older but is still struggling in constant battles over control, therapists and parents have to work from that child's psychosocial developmental level. That will allow the child to work through the stage, develop the virtue needed and move forward. For older children that have been adopted, adoption can also cause regressions in behavior that open up opportunities for a child to work on previous traumas and missed stages. When a child is able to work through each stage, their self-image and values will also continue to develop. Their self-concept will develop in a more securely attached manner, and their ability to see themselves as successful in relationships becomes more of a reality.

Erickson and Piaget combined help us to understand how a child starts to form their identity. The characters of their life story set the stage. Since most children do not have memories consciously from age 0-3, families can use stories to help children understand who they are and where they come from. They can share pictures, favorite foods, baby books, and family memories from events. What many adoptive parents do not realize is how much the birth family's culture and experience has an influence on the child's story and later identity. Even when children are adopted by the same race or ethnic group, a child may struggle because they want to know the stories that led to their birth. Issues like family planning, what the birth parents were doing in their lives, ability to provide, cultural or political issues can all help a child not only learn why adoption was the best option for their birth family but also to accept that their personhood or character was not being rejected by their birth family. A child might be able to start seeing past the loss of "being given up" or the parents "letting them go". So often adoptive families focus on how a child has become a blessed addition to their adoptive family, but we try to avoid the painful reality that they were lost by another family. Helping children see they were a loss to their birth family, they were loved and had an identity, and they are special to both families allows a healthy sense of self to develop. Whether a birth parent did choose adoption for their child willingly or the parent had no capacity to make a choice, every child has value and a place in their birth parent's story. The more a child understands how adoption was the best plan to give the child a family that could love, support, and keep them safe, the more they can start to process how they were not just "given away" or "there were flaws that made them unworthy".

These theories continue to affect development until death and some children grow into adults who never reconcile these basic developmental stages. This is why some children that have been adopted who have behavioral and emotional issues can often find healing with a therapist in adulthood. Their brain, at that point in time, has grown with larger abilities to rationalize their birth story, adoption story, and their self-concept. These theories are essential to how one should parent children that have been adopted because if they have not mastered a stage of development, then they should be parented based on the stage in which they are stuck, not the stage in which they should be based on their chronological age. We would not expect a child who never passed basic reading skills to read Charles Dickens or William Shakespeare, so how can we expect children who maybe never learned to trust to sit through a school day, mind their teacher, and develop social relationships without some major disruptions?

SCHOOL-AGED CHILDREN

When children that have been adopted enter school, they can be anywhere on the continuum of psycho-social development. Some have mastered several stages and are above the curve, and others feel like they are still stuck trying to figure out if they are even safe. Even if they are on target academically, meeting developmental milestones at the pediatrician's office, and "fitting in" with the rest of the family, children process who they are in the world intentionally at each one of Erikson's developmental phases. It can be hard to tell where children that have been adopted are on that continuum. Generally, where children operate out of the majority of the time is where a child is going to best be processing their story. For example, if a child is seven, was adopted at age four, and is playing and interacting with children at the age of five more appropriately and developmentally on target than children at the age of seven, we would assume the child is more developmentally at age five rather than seven. He or she, at times, may even present like a two or three-year-old if they are throwing a tantrum, but the stage of psycho-social development they will be working on is that of the five-year-old (the

Preschool Phase). Parents would be helping them most with trying to develop their sense of purpose, but they might also have to first work on making sure the child knows they are safe if the child is regressed at various points. Parents have to be self-aware enough to see how their own attachment styles are being affected by their child's behavior. Children with Reactive Attachment tendencies will be able to "push their parent's buttons" to test them and see if they will snap or reject them. If they can make the parent upset, it confirms to them that parents are not safe people. This delicate dance is often seen in children with low socio-emotional development because they want to see if they are safe. They are testing the reality of the objects/caregivers in their life, and they almost always have no awareness that they are doing this. This is because the concept of safety and security is developed at a preverbal/preconscious stage. Therapists in the adoption field are starting to recognize that trying to treat behaviors and even thought patterns generally does not improve behaviors in this area for children that have been adopted. These children are starting to get more dramatic results with therapies that work with unconscious thoughts and pre-verbal trauma memories like Eye Movement Desensitization and Reprocessing (EMDR) therapy.

Therapeutic holding was used for many years and is still used in some situations with children that have been adopted. What research found was that many of these children had violent reactions to being touched when they were upset because during their emotional breakdowns the child had regressed and felt unsafe. They did not trust the adoptive parent and being touched could trigger floods of emotions of physical abuse or neglect. Some children who resisted and fought touch for hours would eventually surrender in exhaustion rather than because they felt safe. Forced surrender is not the same as safety. When adoptive parents create additional traumas by trying to solve a behavioral issue without considering the psycho-social stage of their child, they risk reinforcing the child's sense of being unsafe. Again, the child fails to learn to trust in that infancy stage, but if the adoptive parent can therapeutically meet an angry and scared child in a way that brings security, they can change and rewrite the child's understanding of their safety in the world; the child's narrative of the world changes.

As a child reprocesses Erickson's stages in therapy with their caregiver, they shift from chronic feelings of danger to safety. They develop a healthier self-concept and relationship with others because it is as if they are re-training the brain how to interpret social interactions. They are also re-training their own emotional responses to others. These opportunities often happen every day through a consistent routine, a non-emotional response from a parent when a child makes a mistake, nurturing, and the parent helping the child to see their strengths. The parent's verbal and non-verbal feedback rewrite the child's narrative from "I am unsafe, scared, isolated, and don't fit in" to "I am loved, I am safe, I have a family, and I am important". This process is far from simple. It is a long-term adjustment of trying to repair old wounds while simultaneously growing up and adjusting to the age-appropriate challenges they face. It is always important for adoptive parents to remember that while they have a child whose birth certificate says one age, they have adopted a child who is actually, often times, a much younger age emotionally. The phrase "age is just a number" should be applied in a relationship with an adoptive child from how you care for them, talk to them, and what information to share about their birth story at different stages.

Often in therapy, adoptive parents struggle with this concept. There before their eyes is a beautiful school-aged child who seems so smart, on target, sometimes even overly mature, but then their thinking skills, social behavior, and logic feel like that of a preschooler. The parent can get frustrated and angry with the child, thus creating further stress to the child who is attempting to master the stage of Initiation versus Guilt. This child may be exploring and testing, but if their parent figure does not allow this to take place, the child will develop a large sense of guilt and will not confidently move on to the school-aged phase with a sense of purpose in the world. The more of Erikson's phases that are interrupted and struggled through, the poorer and poorer the child's self-concept develops.

There is a child late into elementary school who is starting to dress dramatically with more teenage style clothes and sneaking behind her parents' backs with sexual behaviors, cursing, and more teenage-like behavior. Her interests however at home can also be misleading as she often watches cartoons, makes poor social choices with her peers, and has very little empathy or remorse for her poor choices. Here is a child who is functioning at more of an emotionally preschool level. The key to noticing this is her social skills. She has no empathy for anyone, she lies, and she is very self-centered. She loves to be the center of attention and her dramatic self-appearance almost resembles a young preschooler wearing a princess gown to school. She is reckless with her anger and often wants to hit others instead of talking when she's angry. She is trying so many adult-like behaviors, it is tempting for her parents to use behavioral modification (removing her electronics and grounding her) to help her make better choices. In a normal developing child, this might work. The child would have values about how other's think and feel about her choices and she would not want to disappoint her parents. For this child, adopted internationally at the age of four, she is completely unaware about these socio-emotional concepts and just feels attacked and angry that her parents are so mean.

Her parents have to scale down the reality of their daughter's emotional development. The child is testing her identity in the world with little ability to use cause and effect thinking about safety. Her parents would benefit from coming to the daughter honoring her desire to learn about the world and herself but educating about boundaries. She is not thinking about what is safe; she is thinking about what feels good and makes her feel loved. She is not thinking about how her choices make her appear to her peers, and most of the time she only seems to care about what she wants for her life. While removing her electronic devices might be a consequence, the emphasis for learning and parenting should be on "how do I let my child start to figure out who she is in the world without making her feel shame and rejection?" While it is more complicated because your child is no longer a preschooler with only access to the things you control, a parent can still guide a teen through this process with forethought and intentionality about this "initiation versus guilt" concept. As long as parents are parenting the children they adopted with these concepts in mind, they will be teaching and helping their child develop the stage-appropriate values they need to function in relationships. This is why adoptive parenting looks nothing like typical parenting, and for families who have birth children, it further complicates the system because adopted children will continue to fail using standard parenting methods. The reality is they just are not ready to be parented to their chronological age.

YOUNG ADULTS

Just as with the other stages, once a child that has been adopted reaches young adulthood, there is no telling where they will be developmentally. For children adopted late into their teen years, a delayed start to development is not uncommon. It is essential for adoptive parents to have a child know and understand their life story prior to adolescence. With as much information as a family can provide or infer based on their adoption agency, research about the culture, open adoption visits, pictures, and other "artifacts" from the child's life, adoptive parents are the guides that help their child interpret the data. Adoptive parents help children "reframe" perceptions of the data to more of a realistic picture that accurately represents the child and their adoption process.

Language is key. Telling a child that has been adopted, "your mom was poor and could not take care of you so she put you up for adoption" infers a child had little meaning and saw the child as an object or even a burden. Whereas, saying, "your mother had a really hard choice to make because she wanted to care for you and love you but did not know how to do that without any money. She chose to search for an adoptive family and made the choice of our family, so that we could take care of you for her. Your mom did not want you to hurt, be hungry, or go without. She made the hardest decision any mother can make for their child". While adoptive families may have never met the birth families, basic concepts about love are true for almost all parent/child relationships. Adoptive parents have to use their own empathy skills to imagine what it was like for the birth family to lose their child. These are moments that are key for adoptees to recognize their worth. When they see the pain their adoptive parents express on behalf of the birth families, the adoptee can start to rewrite any negative self-talk about themselves being unloved, unwanted, and unimportant.

Some adoption stores are not as selfless on paper. Some birth parents do not make a choice; some birth parents hurt their children. This is where externalizing a birth parent's mental health, culture, ignorance or substance abuse is so important because these stories do not fit the mold of a selfless decision or unconditional love. Therapists can be great helpers for families looking to help their children understand their life story. Adoptive parents often know information that makes it difficult to empathize with the birth parents. They are angry because they see how the birth parent's choices impacted the child. Some adoptive families I have worked with who adopted internationally from orphanages almost have a hatred for their child's birth parents and the terrible things they did to their child. This is a barrier for the child to find their positive self-concept because children that have been adopted sense something is wrong, but they do not understand the anger and the emotions towards the birth parents. Often, they internalize those emotions on themselves and see the rejection of the birth parents as a rejection of who they are. This is especially true for children who are transracially adopted, as children's rigid concrete thinking skills lead them to assume that if the adoptive family rejects individual people who are one race, nationality, or group that the child is a part of, then the adoptive family must hate or see them as lesser than as well. While it can be hard to relay acceptance of questionable cultural practices and child rearing ideologies, it is so important for adoptive families not to have a "better than them" mentality when presenting information about the birth family.

Children will have several "seasons" where they reprocess their life story. This is a good sign and shows a child has hit another psycho-social stage. Children will have these phases usually every one-to-three years as they grow and change, so it is important to think of their life story as an organic process that will require ongoing support. The use of a Life Book that belongs to the child, a journal, and art mediums are great ways for young adults to express who they are during this process. While a Life Book often starts as facts, figures, and simple symbols to a young child who wants to know their "facts", they can evolve into a beautiful narrative filled with twists and turns as a child grows and adds more meaning and details to their story. Life Books can show a wide continuum of good and evil, safety and fear, and love and hatred. It is so important for adoptees to have the freedom to look at their stories in a variety of ways and experience who they are, who they were and where they come from. Adoptive parents have such a unique role as they are parents, but they are far more. They are story tellers, guides, teachers, coaches, writers, and safe places. Each day you wake up with your adoptive child is just a step in a journey to them figuring out who they are. You will be the one they think of when they reach certain milestones and they look backward. They will see where you have lead them and taught them to love themselves and others. That is what secure attachment looks like.

Further Implications

While it can be easy for many to see how having their birth information can help one's self-identity form, there is another side of the coin of when a young adult finds out they are adopted after years of constructing an identity with their adoptive family. While this was much more common decades ago before parties involved with adoption were truly aware of how impactful adoption is to a child's story, it unfortunately still happens today. The following is a personal testimony of a friend of mine who gave permission to use this essay in this chapter of the book. While as a clinician, I could support why a child should or could benefit from their birth family's information, her personal journey shared so many of the general themes that many adoptees experience. While her story has a semi-happy ending, she still experiences concern, fear, anxiety, and anger about how her life story has played out.

It is now 2015, I found out that I was adopted in 2007. Finding out that I was adopted at the age of twenty-one, in the middle of my college career threw my life upside down. Prior to finding out, I had a pretty typical relationship with my parents, though they were divorced. I loved them, we got along alright. The day I found out, I was a girl coming home for Christmas break from college ready to share family time with her parents, excited to see her dogs and friends. I left to return to school feeling betrayed. There are so many words that came to mind the day I found out, the weeks following, and even to this day; betrayal is just one of them. I felt angry, upset, lost, pissed, and lied to for twenty-one years! How could my family lie to me for that long?

I feel like my identity that I had grown to know, the facts that you memorize about yourself were no longer true. Hi, my name is _____, my mother is _____ and my father is _____. I have no siblings, raised an only child. I have blue eyes and brown hair. But then you question, EVERYTHING. Who named me? Who were my birth parents? Did I have siblings? Where was I from? Who did I look like? **My identity was stolen from me.**

Since 2007 I have been creating a new identity and story for myself. One that includes people that will accept me for who I am. I am not embarrassed to be who I am and to share my story. I believe that every child has the right to know if they are adopted. That way the child, has time to process and decide what they want to do with all that information as they grow. They may choose to do nothing with it and live their life the way they have been. They may also decide that at an appropriate age they want to seek out more information and explore their heritage. It is a very important subject to approach, and should be done with delicacy. This is a child's life and a very important time for them. The older I get the more I wish I had found out earlier. I am getting ready to get married, settle down and have children of my own. I don't have any medical history of myself. I am going to have to get tests taken and who knows what else just to make sure that I am ok, to know that I will be bringing my baby into a world without any risks. I only know one side of my birth family, my birth father is unknown. That is scary to me.

I wish I had known all along, that I was given the choice. When I did find out, it was not the right way. I found out through a letter from a girl I didn't know, claiming to be my sister. I had to investigate all by myself. I needed to know more. When I did bring up the subject with my mother, she swore to me that it was not true, that I was not adopted, that I did not have any siblings. I did not believe her; I had read the letter. I pressed her for more information which led to an explosion of emotion and details of how I became her daughter. That is not how any child, teenager, or adult should find out who they are.

I have two sisters that I know of on my birth mother's side. It is crazy the small things that we have in common or how we do things the same. Our gestures are the same, sometimes the way we talk is the same. These are just more people to love me.

I choose now, at the age of 29 to surround myself with anybody who loves and cares for me. It is not about blood, or birth parents vs. adoptive parents. Never make your child choose who to love. My mom and dad did what was best for me. I love them. They are my parents, forever. I'm just lucky enough to have some other people in my life that care about me just as much.

Through an adoptee's life time, they will repeat the stories, their heritage, "their facts" that make them special. They need the whole story even the somewhat messy parts (at the appropriate times), so they can come to terms with their adoption story. From conception to death, people come to develop and know themselves based on their experiences and the stories they hold to be true about themselves. Helping children that have been adopted know their story is part of the special role that adoptive families play. It is not always easy, it is very different than the lives of those who have birth children, but it can help a child have less confusion about who they are.

This in turn allows them to someday find love, develop relationships, and maybe have children.

It is hard to discern what to share and when, which is why having other adoptive families, therapists, teachers, and adoption agencies in your family's life is essential. It is hard to assume feelings of birth families or interpret other cultures. It is also hard to know what cultural aspects apply to your adoptive child. Adoptive families have to have an on-going commitment to learn, experience, and dive into their adoptive child's culture. Whether it is a neighborhood across town or a small village on a tiny island, it is not just a place or a people group; it is the foundation for your child's identity. Helping them at each developmental stage learn more about who they are and where they come from is a balancing act, but with support from other adoptive parents, therapists and your agency, families can really learn how to help their child feel safe, learn, and grow.

References

Ainsworth, M. D. S.; & Bowlby, J. (1991), An ethological approach to personality development. *American Psychologist, 46*, 331-341.

Bergman, M.; Linley, L.; & Fawcus, S. (2004) Randomized controlled trial of skin-to-skin contact from birth versus conventional incubator for physiological stabilization in 1200 to 2199 gram newborns. *Acta Paediatrica 93,* 779-785.

Harlow, H. F. (1959). The nature of love. *American Psychologist, 13,* 573-685.

Lewis, T.; Amini, F.; & Lannon, R. (2000). A general theory of love. New York: Vintage.

McLeod, S. A. (2013). Erik Erikson. Retrieved from *www.simplypsychology.org/Erik-Erikson.html*

Good Mommy, Bad Mommy: The Idealized Biological Mother

Bari Benjamin, LCSW, BCD

Bari Benjamin is a former English teacher turned psychotherapist who practices in Pittsburgh, Pennsylvania. She lives with her husband and her nineteen-year-old adopted daughter originally from Moscow. She is also the stepmom to four adult children. She has published memoir essays in *Adoption Today* and *StepMom* magazines as well as several anthologies and *Chicken Soup of the Soul* books. She is currently working on a book of letters to her daughter.

* * *

Driving home from work one day, my four-year-old daughter piped up from her car seat in the back, "Mama, why did my mommy give me up?" I almost swerved the car.

What to say, what to say. I searched my brain trying to remember what the experts tell us. Got it: The latest advice is not to emphasize how much her biological mother loved her and that is why she abandoned her because that could raise fear about me. If I tell her I love her, does that mean I will leave her too? I recalled the recent conference I had attended on adoption issues. The psychologist from Rutgers University suggested that when our children pose this question (and they will), we ask it right back to get a sense of their fantasies.

"I really don't know, sweetie. Why do you think?"

"I think she got really sick and couldn't take care of me."

I agreed that was a possibility.

That was the beginning of the struggle for both of us: she living with the knowledge that there was nothing to know. No history to wrap her budding identity around. No answers to questions that burn in her soul. Myself accepting that I could not make this better for her.

My daughter had been left in a baby carriage in a train station in Moscow at six months old. In the carriage were also family photos (lost forever in the Russian orphanage - I desperately tried to find them), a blanket, and a rattle. At least that was what I was told. The police found her and carried her to one of the twenty-five orphanages called baby homes in Moscow. There she lived until age two when I travelled halfway across the world and brought her home. Sometimes I imagine the rage and panic she must have felt, not seeing her mama's familiar face. Sometimes I see her baby face all scrunched up with tears, wailing for her mama's protective arms.

As a psychotherapist, I understood she would not have conscious memories of this pre-verbal period, but she could remember the feelings attached to these memories - and those feelings would be conscious. I would experience the depth of these feelings in the years to come. I also wondered about the impact of a disrupted attachment and bonding stage of development. This early stage in infancy, the mirroring between the baby and caretaker, is the beginning of the child's positive self-concept and later ability to form healthy relationships. When the baby cries and mommy responds, this repetition communicates a sense of safety, a message that her needs will be satisfied.

Melanie Klein, the Australian-born child psychoanalyst, born in 1882, is the founder of Object Relations Theory. Although she never completed her bachelor's degree, she spent her life analyzing children during play therapy. She believed that infants internalize into their unconscious psyche representations of Mother. When Mother satisfies her baby's needs, she is experienced as "the good or perfect mommy". If she is not available, she becomes "the bad mommy," the epitome of everything negative. All infants, according to Ms. Klein, split mommy in two at a very early age. If their needs are mainly met with consistency, as the infant grows, she heals that split and is able to view mother as a mixture of good and bad, in other words, gain the ability to tolerate ambivalence. If the split is not healed, the child continues to view people as all good or all bad. This makes for big trouble in future relationships. Initially, a person may be idealized until he/she makes one mistake or reveals a flaw, and then he or she can do no right.

I like to believe that my girl experienced tenderness and comfort the first six months with her Russian mom. After all, the items found in her baby carriage reveal concern for her well-being: a blanket to keep her warm, a rattle to play with, and family photographs for connection. But maybe that is just wishful thinking on my part.

What I do know is that her disrupted attachment and lack of knowledge of her biological mother has affected our relationship quite profoundly. From an early age she would cry, "I don't trust you," if I became annoyed or frustrated with her. I wondered then how she even knew what that meant. It came out so naturally. One day, furious that I had taken her video games because she was not doing her homework, she screamed, "I hate you. You're not my real mom. My real mom wouldn't do that. Take me back to Russia." Through the years, I would hear this cry again and again.

My girl's anger frequently exploded like July Fourth firecrackers as she approached adolescence. It seemed like I had become the bad mommy to her as everything I did incensed her. It went beyond the typical teen disapproval of mom. Her rage was palatable. "I hate you, you bitch," she would scream as she slammed her door hard. …

Several years ago, I developed a support group for moms who have adopted internationally. Mom's Coffee Club provides a safe, confidential environment, where mothers can express all feelings related to parenting their adopted children. We tell all: the joy, the hurt, the anger we sometimes feel, the helplessness. The moms in the group empathized. Their children came from all over the world, but if they had lived in an orphanage, they had one striking thing in common. "I don't get it," one mom said, "She's so angry with me, not my husband, just me."

"Yeah," another agreed, "I want to shriek at her. *I'm not the mother who abandoned you. That wasn't me.*

It made me wonder about Melanie Klein's theory. Was my daughter projecting all her negative feelings about her first mother onto me? Had she somehow switched us up in her psyche? Had her Russian mom become the idealized mommy, the one who could do no wrong? After all, it is easy to fantasize wonderful things about someone you do not really know. We all do that. And I certainly did my share of fantasizing about what my little girl would be like before I met her.

I remember day dreaming about my cuddly, little toddler, who would climb onto my lap and rest her head on my chest, her big brown eyes locked onto mine. I would dress her in frilly, girly clothing and carefully brush her hair into pigtails, placing pink barrettes on the ends. Nothing could have been further from those fantasies. The reality was my daughter stiffened in my arms and frequently pulled away during that first year. I could not get a dress near her and brushing her hair was an uncomfortable ordeal. The difference is I would not reject her or become angry with her because she was different from my fantasies. I would stay the course; struggle with her behaviors, yes, but stay the course.

And struggle I did. As adolescence reached its peak, so did the intensity of her risky behaviors. She was leaving school in the middle of the day and staying out all night; sometimes not knowing where she was left me scared and helpless. We embraced therapy—lots of it, and in time, like a baby's first steps, we wobbled together through the maze of hurt and anger.

I cannot help but wonder if my girl had had information about her biological mother, real facts, and better yet, if she had access to her, maybe she would not have become the "perfect mommy" in her head and me the bad mommy. Maybe both of us could have been experienced more realistically. Maybe the split would not have been quite so jagged.

My girl turned nineteen recently. I do believe a remedy to her splitting has been my unshakable presence in her life for the past seventeen years. No matter what, I always took her back. Even after multiple times of her storming out of our home and calling me crying days later, the door remained open. "I don't know how you do it," friends would say, "Anyone else would have given up by now."

Just the other night, while walking her dog with her, she told me, "You know, mom, when I'm mad at you, I hate you in that moment, but I also know I still love you in that moment."

Ahh, the joy of ambivalence. The split is healing.

Recommended Reading and Further Research

Bailey, J. J.; & Giddens, L. N. (2001). *The Adoption Reunion Survival Guide: Preparing yourself for the search, reunion, and beyond.* Oakland, CA: New Harbinger Publications.

Bauer, A. (2008). *The Sound of Hope: A true story of an adoptee's quest for her origins.* Bloomington, IN: iUniverse.

Brodzinsky, D. M.; Schecter, M. D.; & Henig, R. M. (1993). *Being Adopted: The lifelong search for self.* New York, NY: Anchor Books.

Brown, B. (2015). *Rising Strong.* NY, NY: Spiegel & Grau.

Christian, D. R. (2012). *An-ya and Her Diary.* CreateSpace Independent Publishing.

Christian, D. R. & Ellerman, M. A. (Eds.) (2014). *Dear Wonderful You, Letters to Adopted & Fostered Youth.* CreateSpace Independent Publishing.

Christian, D. R.; Gonzalez, R.; & Woolston, A. H. T. (Eds.) (2015). *Flip the Script: Adult adoptee anthology.* CreateSpace Independent Publishing.

Christian, D. R. & Transue-Woolston, A. H. L. (Eds.) (2013). *Perpetual Child: Adult adoptee anthology: dismantling the stereotype.* CreateSpace Independent Publishing.

CLOSURE. Prod. Bryan A. Tucker. Fob & Dongle Productions LLC., 2013. DVD.

Dennis, L. M. (2012). *Adopted Reality: A memoir.* Los Angeles, CA: Entourage Publishing.

Dennis, L. M. (Ed.) (2014). *Adoption Reunion in the Social Media Age: An anthology.* Los Angeles, CA: Entourage Publishing.

Dennis, L. M. (Ed.) (2014). *Adoption Therapy: Perspectives from clients and clinicians on processing and healing post-adoption issues.* Los Angeles, CA: Entourage Publishing.

Eldridge, S. (1999). *Twenty Things Adopted Kids Wish Their Adoptive Parents Knew.* Crystal Lake, IL: Delta.

Eldridge, S. (2007). *Forever Fingerprints: An amazing discovery for adopted children.* Warren, NJ: EMK Press.

Eldridge, S. (2009). *Twenty Things Adoptive Parents Need to Succeed: Discover the unique need of your adopted child and become the best parent you can.* Crystal Lake, IL: Delta.

Eske, A. (2010). *My Family, A Symphony: A memoir of global adoption.* New York, NY: Palsgrave MacMillan.

Goldman, C. & Bond, J. C. (2015). *Jazzy's Quest: Adopted and amazing!* Jacksonville, FL: Marcinson Press.

Gritter, J. L. (2009). *Hospitious Adoption.* Washington, DC: Child & Family Press.

Grubb, L. (Ed.) (2015). *The Adoptee Survival Guide: Adoptees share their wisdom and tools.* CreateSpace Independent Publishing.

Hill, R. (2012). *Finding Family: My search for roots and the secrets in my DNA.* CreateSpace Independent Publishing.

Holden, L. (2013). *The Open-Hearted Way to Open Adoption: Helping your child grow up whole.* Lanham, MD: Rowman & Littlefield.

Keefer, B. & Schooler, J. E. (2000). *Telling the Truth to Your Adopted or Foster Child: Making sense of the past.* Bergin & Garvey Trade.

Lifton, B. J. (1995). *Journey of The Adopted Self: A quest for wholeness.* New York, NY: Basic Books.

O'Connor, S. H. (2012). *The Harris Narratives: An introspective study of a transracial adoptee.* Cambridge, MA: The Pumping Station.

Palmer, C. (2016). *An Affair with My Mother: A story of adoption, secrecy and love.* Dublin: Penguin Ireland.

Pavao, J. M. (2005). *The Family of Adoption: Completely revised and updated.* Boston, MA: Beacon Press.

Sayre, J. E. (2016). *My secret: The true story of one woman's adoption discovery and search.* Joanne E. Sayre.

Schooler, J. E. & Norris, B. L. (2002). *Journeys after Adoption: Understanding lifelong issues.* Santa Barbara, CA: Praeger.

Shrodes, D. D. (2014). *Worthy to be Found: An unforgettable story of reunion, resilience, and restoration.* Los Angeles, CA: Entourage Publishing.

Steffen, C. A. (2014). *A Family Apart - Sleuthing the Mysteries of Abandonment, Adoption and DNA - A memoir.* Dayton, OH: Greyden Press.

Swift, G. H. & Swift, C. A. (2013). *ABC, Adoption & Me — A multi-cultural picture book for adoptive families.* Gayle Swift.

Transue-Woolston, A. H. L.; Stromberg, J.; Pickell, K.; & Anastasi, J. (Eds.) (2014). *Lost Daughters: Writing adoption from a place of empowerment and peace.* CQT Media And Publishing.

Verrier, N. (2004) *Coming Home to Self: The adopted child grows up.* Nancy Verrier.

Verrier, N. (1993) *The Primal Wound: Understanding the adopted child.* Baltimore, MD: Gateway.

Editor's note: This list is a compilation made from the authors. I have not read each of these books, and I cannot specifically recommend them. All of them look interesting, and I hope they present these topics in a positive light.